EXTRAORDINARY DOGS

*True-life stories and the science behind
the remarkable abilities of man's best friend*

Text by Elizabeth Wilhide

Quadrille
PUBLISHING

Introduction

Our relationship with dogs has been a long and rewarding one, stretching back over many thousands of years. Although it's fair to say that dogs have hugely benefited from their association with humans, arguably we have got the better deal. We have depended on dogs for their superior powers in so many ways – for their strength and endurance to assist us in opening up new territories for colonization, for their protection and companionship, as fleet-footed, agile and acutely sensed partners in the hunt for food, and as courageous defenders in the battle against predators. Over the course of many centuries, through selective breeding, we have shaped them to our ends, the better to fulfil our needs. Collies to herd sheep at whistled commands, Huskies to pull a sled bringing much-needed supplies and mountain breeds that guard livestock are but the many varied faces of Dog.

Today, most domestic dogs, purebred or not, are pets. They are fed, walked, stroked and cherished as family members. They are micro-chipped, vaccinated and taken to the vet for regular check-ups and, through our intervention, they undoubtedly lead longer, healthier, safer and more pampered lives than ever before. This is not surprising given how much we value the joy dogs bring to our lives. But often little more is asked of them than to be the passive recipients of our care.

Yet, as the stories in this book remind us, dogs are capable of much greater feats than we know or can fully understand. In exceptional circumstances – in the aftermath of earthquakes and avalanches, for example – their powers of detection can save lives. In times of need – assisting those who are disabled – they have proved sensitive guides to independence. And in times of crisis they confound us with their remarkable loyalty and apparent sixth sense.

Such dogs may seem super-heroes of the canine world. While it is true that some dogs possess really remarkable capabilities that can be honed and shaped by expert training, all dogs have something extraordinary about them: resources of strength, sensory awareness, agility and instinct just waiting to be tapped.

Recently, scientists and researchers are beginning to discover what lies behind some of these extraordinary powers and, in the process, to gain a better understanding of just what makes dogs tick. The surprising answer, in many cases, is that dogs love to learn and love to work. When set a task, even a seemingly impossible one, they will marshal their unique abilities and rise to the challenge, often exceeding our expectations by the widest of margins.

Humans originally bred dogs to be their working companions. That instinct lies deep within their nature. For dogs, it's all about playing the game. Train your dog, keep teaching it new tricks and setting it new challenges, and you will begin to appreciate just how much it can do and how far it can go.

TRAINING

Imagine you were born with an incredible aptitude for drawing, or playing music or solving mathematical problems. Yet, from childhood onwards, no one provided you with the opportunity to exercise those talents: no paints or crayons, no musical instruments, no sums to do. No matter

how well you were cared for and loved, you would be frustrated and bored.

The same is true of dogs that aren't given the chance to exercise their physical and mental skills. While this book does not set out to be a practical training manual for dog owners, many of the stories featured here indicate just how much dogs can do if they receive the right guidance and teaching, even as adults. If you are inspired by the remarkable feats described in this book, why not give your dog the chance to rise to the occasion? It's never too late for a dog to learn.

Training a dog takes a lot of time and patience, but the rewards are great for both owner and dog alike. Basic obedience training is all very well and good, and teaches a dog to live in our world. Set your dog bigger challenges, and you will start to release its full potential.

Communication skills

Teaching a dog to respond to simple one-word spoken commands is the basis of dog training. Here, consistency is very important: say 'sit' every time you want the dog to sit, not 'down' or 'sit down', for example. At the same time, in certain circumstances dogs are much more responsive to hand gestures and movement than the spoken word. Pairing a command with a gesture means you can communicate with your dog over a greater distance.

Positive reinforcement

During training, all dogs will make mistakes and it may take many lessons and a lot of practice before they can perform on cue. Don't discipline a dog for failure: just ignore the occasions when it fails to do what it is supposed to do. When it performs correctly, offer praise, encouragement and other types of reward. Food treats should be used in moderation. The type of play that addresses a dog's natural instincts is far more effective as an incentive to learn.

Variety is the spice of life

Like humans, dogs need variety. The same game of 'fetch' in the same park every day won't offer much in the way of stimulation. Variety is also essential to bed down training. Whatever the command, teach your dog to respond to it in different locations so that it doesn't just associate the instruction with a particular place or circumstance. Begin training in quiet areas indoors that don't offer much in the way of distraction and then proceed to more challenging environments where your dog has to concentrate harder to pay attention.

Play to your dog's strengths

While all dogs share a number of basic characteristics, selective breeding has brought certain traits to the fore in specific breeds. When training your dog, play to its strengths so you satisfy its innate drives and exploit its capabilities. Remember, too, that whatever the breed, all dogs are individuals.

'As we uncover more and more about the extraordinary ways in which dogs can assist us in many aspects of our lives, in both illness and good health, only then will we truly see just how remarkable their abilities are and appreciate them even more.'

DAVID MORGAN

'Dogs are the only species to have evolved in a working relationship with humans and that places them in a very special and important position within our modern society.'

DAVID MORGAN EUKANUBA SCIENTIFIC
COMMUNICATION MANAGER AND CANINE EXPERT

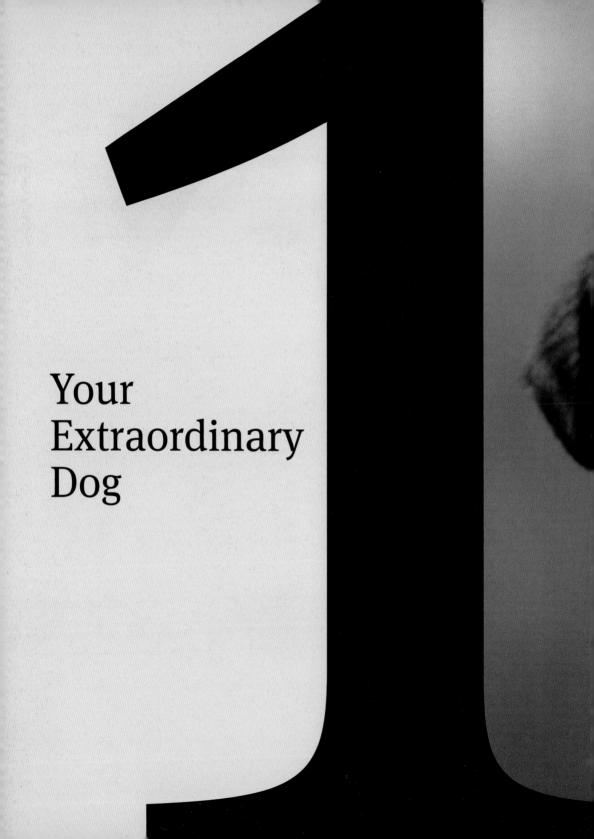

Your
Extraordinary
Dog

Your Extraordinary Dog

Dogs may share 99.8% of their genetic make-up with wolves, but they aren't wolves. They may share our lives, mimic our behaviour, read our body language like a book – sometimes knowing what makes us tick even better than we know ourselves – but they aren't humans, either, however much we may be tempted to anthropomorphize them.

Dogs are dogs. And each and every one of them is extraordinary. Yet as the stories in this book reveal, some are even more extraordinary than others.

The relationship between dogs and humans, which stretches back thousands of years – at least 15,000 years, perhaps earlier, according to some theories – is the closest example of cross-species collaboration and bonding in the animal kingdom. From the outset the two species learned to pool their efforts. With early humans using tools and weapons and dogs contributing their superior sense of smell to the chase, the two species proved to be much more efficient hunters working in partnership than alone.

For many, many centuries, dogs and humans have continued to work alongside each other, surviving often harsh and difficult circumstances. While the dog's unique capabilities of sensory awareness, strength, stamina and agility have served us well, as in any relationship, dogs have benefited too. We have provided them with a reliable source of food, for one thing, which may well have been one of the factors that spurred the process of domestication.

What we know about the origins of dogs tells us they are highly social animals. As such, they are a perfect fit with humans, who similarly organize themselves in families and loose community groups. Throughout history, dogs have been always been valued for their companionship as much as their working skills. Today, most dogs around the world – of which there are many millions – are pets, part and parcel of family life.

For years, very little research was carried out into dog behaviour, as it was felt that dogs had almost nothing to teach us. Happily over a decade ago this began to change and we now live in an era when never before has so much scientific time and expertise been devoted to the study of our four-legged friends. This has hugely benefited our relationship with them.

Daniel Mills, Professor of Veterinary Behavioural Medicine at Lincoln University, is a leading academic in the field of animal behaviour. He is passionate about conveying the message that just as dogs are not humans, neither are they wolves. 'The dog itself is a wonderful thing. To get the most from your own dog, you need to understand it for the animal it is. People have interpreted the pack system, for example, as hierarchical. In fact we now know that it is much more of a family system. You won't get the most from a dog by dominating it – you always need to build up a relationship with it, so that it becomes your good friend who wants to please you.'

Sight

The eyes of the Hungarian Vizsla (*left*) and the White Swiss Shepherd (*right*) are set more towards the sides of their heads, giving them a wide field of vision.

The dog has inherited many of its traits from its wolf ancestors and its sense of sight is no exception. For the wolf, keen discriminatory vision is vital to spot the movements of prey over the long expanses of open ground where it hunts. An ability to see in dim conditions also helps the wolf track prey at dusk and dawn, its preferred time for hunting.

A dog's sense of sight is very different from our own. Our vision is binocular and forward-directed, while the dog's is more monocular, or peripheral, allowing them to detect the slightest movement – even when that movement is coming fom behind them.

This capability is one of the reasons why dogs make such good guides for the visually impaired. They can literally keep an eye on every hazard and obstacle that surrounds them.

FIELD OF VISION

Our eyes, placed at the front of our heads, give us a field of vision of about 180 degrees. We have to turn if we want to see things that are to the side of us or behind us. That's not true of dogs. The positioning of their eyes at the sides of their heads gives them a much wider field of vision, between 250 and 260 degrees. Even where the anatomy of a particular breed narrows that visual field somewhat (owing to the size of the snout or shape of the skull), all dogs have much better peripheral vision than humans. In the case of 'sight hounds', such as Greyhounds and Whippets, the field of vision massively exceeds our own.

Humans take in their surroundings using long sweeping glances. Our eyes make many unconscious movements back and forth to allow us to fill our 'blind spots' with images we think should be there. Although dogs lack the same capability, this gives them a distinct advantage in some circumstances. Rather than filling gaps in their visual field with what they think should be there, dogs only take in details that are actually present, which means they are less likely to overlook what matters.

CRYSTAL CLEAR

Unlike some mammals, dogs also possess a third eyelid, which helps to keep the visual field crystal clear. Common in birds and reptiles, the third eyelid – or nictitating membrane – is a thin strip of cartilage covered by a membrane whose job is to keep the surface of the eye lubricated and protected.

TAKING A DIM VIEW

In conditions of low light a dog's eyesight particularly excels: a dog can see an object at a light threshold six times lower than a human would need to see the same thing. The reason for this is a special light-reflecting layer at the backs of their eyes called the *tapetum lucidum*.

Many people think that dogs are colour-blind, but this is not the case. However, it is true that they do not have such an acute sense of colour as we do, and find it difficult to differentiate red from green. They also tend to be short-sighted. Most dogs can only focus objects within 50cm to 30cm of the eye. And three breeds – the German Shepherd, the Rottweiler and the Miniature Schnauser – have a high prevalence of myopia (short sight).

Hearing

An Australian Kelpie (*left*) and a lively Cairn Terrier (*right*) have their ears pricked up and facing forward, alert to sounds coming from straight ahead.

Imagine what it would be like to hear a mouse squeak many metres away. Like sight and smell, hearing is another canine super-sense, part of a dog's natural biological make-up. Before dogs were domesticated their acute sense of hearing helped them to survive in the wild by tracking the sounds made by both prey and predators. Now their superior audio recognition is being put to use to assist human companions who are hearing impaired.

We've all seen dogs prick up their ears at sounds we are unable to detect. Some of us may even have used a 'silent' dog whistle to train or call our pets – 'silent' to us, that is! Dogs hear far better than humans. They hear sounds over a greater range of frequencies, they hear sounds much further away and they can pinpoint the origins of those sounds with an exceptional degree of accuracy.

'Dogs can localize a sound and accurately pinpoint where it's coming from in as little as 0.06 of a second – that's very different from humans.'

DAVID MORGAN, CANINE EXPERT

RANGE

The dog's ability to hear across a wide range of frequencies opens up a whole world of sound to them that we simply can't hear. Dogs can detect sounds as low as 67 Hz – the equivalent of thunder rumbling in the distance – much the same as we can. But their high frequency hearing is far superior to ours and extends right up to 45,000 Hz, which is ten times higher than a soprano hitting top C. (The human range extends only up to 23,000 Hz.) With such sensitive hearing this means that even when dogs are sleeping they can pick up noises that are inaudible to us.

DISTANCE AND DIRECTION

Dogs' distance hearing is ten times better than ours; a sound that we can hear at a distance of 20 metres, a dog can pick up 200 metres away. And within some part of their hearing range they can pinpoint the precise origin of a sound at a distance about four times further than we can.

Like dogs, our ears are on each side of our heads. Unlike dogs, we can't move them. If we want to tell accurately where a sound is coming from, we have to turn or move our heads.

A dog's directional hearing is very different. Because a dog's ears are large and moveable, it can localize a sound to a high degree of accuracy and it can do this fast – in about one-sixhundredth of a second. More than eighteen separate muscles pivot, tilt, elevate or lower the ear, ensuring that dogs know which direction potential danger is coming from. But it doesn't stop there. Deeper down, in the middle part of the structure of the ear, there's a small but very important muscle composed of special fibres. It is believed that possession of these rare fibres found in canine species – fibres that contract extremely quickly – is one of the reasons why dogs can hear frequencies far above the capabilities of the human ear.

Smell

A dog's world is almost entirely organized by smell. Their amazing scent-detecting powers are so far superior to ours as to make them almost incomprehensible to us. It's as if they experience an entirely different dimension altogether.

A few facts serve to illustrate just how extraordinary the dog's sense of smell truly is. Whereas we have about 5 million scent receptor cells in our noses, dogs have up to 200 million – in tracking breeds, such as bloodhounds, for example, that number may be as great as 300 million. This gives dogs the ability to differentiate between a million individual scent patterns, compared to our ability to distinguish a mere thousand. Dogs can also detect odours at concentrations many times lower than we can.

In the wild, a dog's highly developed sense of smell enabled them to track down prey, avoid predators and identify other members of its pack. Although sight and hearing have also played a part in the survival of the species, the importance of smell has been paramount. As Daniel Mills, Professor of Veterinary Behavioural Medicine, Lincoln University, explains: 'In order for dogs to feed, they needed to be able to track prey over long distances, to search

out food when they couldn't necessarily see it. It's not the same for a horse, for example, where grass is readily available and there's no need to hunt for it.'

SNIFFING THE AIR

When a dog wants to sniff the surrounding air for odours, it is able to take in the air through dilated (widened) nostrils. This greater volume of air passes to the parts of the nasal cavity where the olfactory (scent) receptors are more numerous. And they can ventilate this area with a constant stream of air entering via the nostrils in spite of breathing out. Breathing in and out through the nose, as we tend to do, limits the amount of olfactory information we can take in.

Dogs' noses are famously wet, thanks to their tear ducts, which run all the way down to the end of the nose. There are good reasons for this. A wet nose allows dogs to feel from which direction the wind is blowing and thus sniff out the scents carried on the breeze. The moisture in the nasal cavity also helps dissolve scent molecules so the receptor cells located in the nose can pick up specific odours.

SCENT-PROCESSING

When a dog sniffs an odour, the scent passes via the nostrils to the nasal membranes, which overlay an area of thin bones in the nose. These bones have intricate creases, ensuring that even the smallest scent molecules are captured. In a Labrador, for example, the nasal membranes may amount to as much as a square metre of olfactory surface tissue. Once the membranes have captured a scent, sensory cells change it to an electro-chemical message and send it to the brain.

Because humans navigate by sight, we have

While hunting dogs like the German Long-haired Pointing Dog (*top*) have good scenting abilities, scent hounds such as the Grand Bleu de Gascogne (*bottom*) have among the most sensitive noses of all dogs.

a large visual cortex in the brain where this information is processed. In dogs, it is their olfactory cortex, with 40 times as many of the brain cells involved in deciphering odours as humans, which is highly developed.

What's even more amazing is that sensations picked up by a dog's whiskers are also routed to the same olfactory centre in the brain – so in a sense dogs 'smell' with their whiskers as well as their nose. In addition, dogs have a special scent-detecting organ in the roof of their mouth, the vomeronasal organ, which in humans is thought not to have the same complex function in detecting chemical pheromones.

'Textbooks will tell you that a dog's sense of smell is between 1,000 and 10,000 times more sensitive than ours. For certain molecules that sensitivity can increase to up to a 100 million times greater.'

DAVID MORGAN, CANINE EXPERT

'Dogs have a very large olfactory surface area in their noses. They also have a scent-detecting organ in the roof of their mouths that humans lack. Dogs pick up scent in a completely different way than we do and one that is truly incomprehensible to us.'

BRUCE FOGLE, CANINE EXPERT

Strength and Stamina

The giant size and tremendous strength of Newfoundlands (*left*) is combined with a calm, affectionate disposition; the Uruguayan Cimarron (*right*), another large, muscular breed, combines strong physique with strong temperament.

While dogs vary hugely in height, weight, appearance and behaviour, their relatively powerful muscles, combined with certain anatomical adaptations, enable them to perform feats of remarkable strength and endurance. Larger breeds, in particular, bred for working purposes, exhibit a great deal of staying power. One of the largest breeds, the Newfoundland, can swim long distances and resist strong tides thanks to its big lung capacity and large skeleton. Sledding dogs such as Alaskan Huskies can regularly pull two to three times their own body weight.

Ever since the dawn of domestication, humans have relied on the superior strength and stamina of dogs for their own survival – even for the colonization of new territories. It is thought, for example, that early migrants from Siberia to North America relied on sled dogs to transport them across the Bering Strait.

TUG OF WAR

As natural predators, dogs have jaws and teeth adapted for grasping, pulling and tearing, as anyone who has ever played a game of tug with their pet will testify. The bite strength of dogs, which for large breeds can vastly exceed our own, is an invaluable asset in rescue work.

GOING THE DISTANCE

Dogs are capable of going long distances over significant periods of time, a trait they are thought to have acquired from their wolf ancestors, who engaged in extensive chases after prey. Today, on long working sessions, dogs demonstrate the same incredible degree of stamina. This owes much to the fact that the steady rate at which they cover the ground is not so fast as to exceed their energy reserves. Their heat-loss mechanisms, such as panting, also serve to offset the heat that is generated by muscular activity, thus maintaining a balanced core temperature.

EXTREME CONDITIONS

Working alongside humans, dogs have encountered extreme conditions and inhospitable environments, from snowy wastes to tropical jungles. How do they cope?

Part of the answer lies in their cardiovascular system. Dogs have an interesting adaptation of the blood vessels supplying the brain, which helps them if they are working in hot conditions. When the core body temperature rises, hot blood is shunted away from the brain, keeping it cool. In cold weather, on the other hand, the circulation system of the dog acts as a heat exchange. Warm blood carrying oxygen to the limbs flows in arteries right alongside the veins carrying blood in the opposite direction. This allows heat to be transferred to the cooler blood travelling up from the extremities.

TURBO-CHARGED

For energy, humans are largely reliant on starches and sugars – carbohydrates – which are stored in the body in the form of glycogen. When we take part in strenuous exercise, we start to metabolize these glycogen reserves until the point when we begin to suffer fatigue and eventually have to come to a stop. Only when glycogen stores are replenished can we really carry on and perform well again.

Dogs, however, are different. Their muscle metabolism enables them to keep on going when they are working hard or moving fast. Rather than only metabolizing carbohydrates, under the stress of exertion they are able to switch to metabolizing fat, which provides over twice as much energy gramme for gramme as does carbohydrate. Canine muscle tissue is more adept at getting energy from fat than human muscle.

Movement

As anyone who has ever let their dog off the lead in a park or open space and watched it race off into the distance at high speed knows, dogs are hard-wired for movement. More to the point, they seem to relish their speed and agility, clearing obstacles with centimetres to spare, leaping up to catch balls and Frisbees, doubling back time and again to cover more than twice as much ground as you do. Deep in the genetic ancestry of dogs, these traits ensured their survival as predators and made them successful hunters.

For our domestic dogs, exercise is one really important stress-buster. In their working lives, the opportunities to exercise such physical skills also prove a reward in themselves.

Some breeds, such as Border Collies, bred to herd sheep at speed as part of their nature, need regular and lengthy work-outs far and above the requirements of the average pooch. Greyhounds and Whippets, on the other hand, the sprinters of the canine world, can make do with much shorter bursts of activity.

AGILITY

As natural hunters, dogs have evolved to be very agile, which helps them to cope with a wide variety of different terrains where the ground may be irregular. Their sure-footedness has proved an obvious advantage in allowing them to track down their prey and escape from their predators.

Four legs and splayed paws give dogs a great sense of balance. They're also able to shift their body weight at speed, which helps them tackle the obstacles encountered on rough ground by jumping, haring round corners, and racing up and down steep inclines.

SPEED

Dogs bred for running, such as Greyhounds and Whippets, can reach speeds of 55 kmph, which makes them one of the fastest land animals. By comparison the top speed of the average non-athletic human is about 24 kmph.

These fast breeds of dog have a number of adaptations that help them reach such high speeds. For example, they have proportionately larger hearts, which deliver more oxygen-rich blood to their muscles.

POWERHOUSE

In dogs, it is their strong hindquarters – in particular, their hamstring muscles – that generate most of the power they need for fast movement. Canine muscles, such as those in the hind limbs, are large and long, which makes them very powerful.

The dog's unique biomechanics also has a bearing on its power of movement, as canine expert John Innes, Professor of Small Animal Surgery, University of Liverpool, explains:

An enthusiastic runner, bred to chase hares and rabbits, the Beagle (*top*) displays tremendous agility at speed, while the Alaskan Malamute (*bottom*), bred as a sled dog, combines speed with strength.

'Humans stand with their heels on the ground and their knees relatively straight. If you look at the canine hind limb, the hock (or heel) is off the ground and the knee is flexed most of the time. Dogs are able to store energy in certain muscles and tendons, using them almost like springs during motion.'

Dogs also lack a collarbone and their shoulder joints are unable to rotate as our shoulders can. This means their gait is typically forward-directed, with very little energy wasted on movement up and down.

Breeds
Apart

Breeds Apart

'Breeds of dogs can differ by over one hundred times in their body weight; no other species has such diversity.' DAVID MORGAN, CANINE EXPERT

From the tiny Chihuahua to the massive Great Dane, no other species of mammal varies so widely in appearance as the domestic dog. Breeds today come in a truly astonishing range of heights and weights, and display significant differences in colouring, coat type, ear shape and facial structure, amongst many other characteristics. But it isn't all about physique. Breeds also have distinctive behaviours and temperaments: just think of the dogged persistence of terriers, the keen intelligence of collies or the easy-going sociability of Labradors.

All domestic dogs are descendants of the grey wolf (*Canis lupus*). Early on in their association with humans, dogs evolved into a number of different types, both as a result of environmental factors such as climate, and the kind of functional roles they were called upon to play. Yet even at this stage humans also manipulated the breeding of their four-legged companions to meet their specific needs. It is not hard to imagine, for example, aggressive individuals being passed over for littermates that displayed more willingness and obedience, or stronger individuals and those that possessed keener senses being preferred over weaker specimens.

Over the centuries, people have actively sought to create dogs with particular traits and still do so today. Often these characteristics had to do with working ability, but appearance and even fashion and status also played a role. Once an understanding of genetics developed, breed numbers really took off and hundreds of different breeds are now recognized.

Opposite, top to bottom Whippet; Bloodhound; Pyrenean Mountain Dog; English Pointer; Jack Russell Terrier; English Toy Terrier.

SIGHT HOUNDS

Breeds such as Whippets and Greyhounds have excellent vision, long necks and long jaws. They hunt by sight, while their muscular body and long legs give them the speed to sprint after the prey they spot on the horizon.

SCENT HOUNDS

Dogs such as Bloodhounds that hunt by ground-scent typically have large noses, deep nostrils and long ears, all characteristics that accentuate their olfactory powers. Built for stamina and endurance, they are capable of tracking an unseen quarry over long distances.

WORKING DOGS

Dogs bred to carry out various specific jobs for their human owners – herding, pulling, guarding and hunting – tend to be big and strong. Some display more specific characteristics that are assets for the work they have to do. Newfoundlands, for example, originally bred to assist fishermen, have waterproof coats and webbing in their feet, which make them good swimmers.

SPORTING DOGS

Unlike scent hounds, sporting dogs hunt by scenting the air. Retrievers, bred to find and return game to the hunter, have soft mouths and willing natures. Pointers indicate the quarry by standing rigid, pointing their nose and body in its direction. Spaniels, who also have keen noses, were originally used to flush game out of the undergrowth.

TERRIERS

This group of small, strong, wiry dogs was originally bred to hunt and kill vermin such as rats. Terriers are typically energetic, determined and a great deal braver than their compact size suggests.

MINIATURE OR TOY BREEDS

Throughout history, most dogs kept by humans have been working companions. Toy breeds, whose diminutive size precludes any real practical role, were early status symbols for the wealthy and privileged.

Alaskan Huskies are a favourite breed for sled-dog racing. Because they are bred for speed they have a longer, leaner physique than other huskies.

'The power comes out of their hind legs and it's all transferred through the harness. When they actually take off it's pretty phenomenal to watch. Their heads go down between their shoulders and everything just goes right on the hind legs.'

CLEMENS BITTENDORFER, MUSHER

RARING TO GO

In Australia's only snow-based sled dog race, a team of Alaskan Huskies show how successful these working dogs, specially bred for speed, can be.

Dinner Plain, a tiny ski village situated above the snowline in the Great Dividing Range in Victoria, southern Australia, is the location of the country's only snow-based sled dog race. For 17 years teams from around the world have been coming here to compete in this tough annual event, where mushers and their dogs race against the clock to see who can complete the challenging course in the fastest possible time.

Clemens Bittendorfer from New South Wales and his team of Alaskan Huskies haven't lost a race in six years. He considers these dogs – thought by many to be a mix of several working dog breeds – ideal for the competition. 'The breed is crazy about working and that's probably the most important factor in their success. They are bred to run, they love to run, and they love to work.'

Perfectly adapted for running fast, all the power generated by their hind legs is directed forward, going into speed, and the oxygen intake of fit sled dogs can be three times higher than an elite cross-country skier. While panting is a dogs' main way of dissipating heat, these dogs have shorter coats than other huskies, which also helps.

Clemens's team consists of littermates Benny, Bjorn and Frida, all aged eight, and Fernando, aged six, from a third generation. During the race the dogs will be pulling two to three times their own body weight.

The dogs spend four months training for the event. 'Our season starts around June,' says Clemens. 'As soon as the temperature drops below 10 degrees or so, I'll start taking them on short runs and let them pull heavy-ish weights to build up their muscles. Then we'll extend the distance and increase the speed.'

Part of the pre-race preparation is to ensure the dogs are hydrated and have the right food intake. Clemens also gives them a rub-down with liniment to warm up their muscles. As they will be running in snowy conditions, it's essential to protect their feet. 'Booties' placed over the paws of the sled dogs prevent snow from building up between their toes.

During the most recent sled dog race, 67 mushers and teams took part. In Clemens's four-dog category, there were 12 other competitors, all as determined to win as he was. The course included a downhill section with quite sharp turns. With a significant snowfall the week before the race, it all added up to quite tough conditions.

With pressure to maintain his unbroken record, stakes were high for Clemens and his team as they entered the first of the timed heats. Much to his delight, and thanks to his dogs' remarkable power and stamina, they finished first in their group. 'It was really hard work,' said Clemens, afterwards. 'The snow was really soft. But the dogs worked so hard, it was fantastic. We finished well, the dogs were happy and it was great.'

STEADY BEAT

Bred for their patience and intelligence,
Labernese dogs like Tartin are helping
Canadian children with autism.

The MIRA Foundation (*Fondation Mira*) is the only accredited centre for training guide and service dogs in Quebec. It's also the place where a special kind of dog is being bred to work with children with autism. The results have been astonishing.

Autism is a developmental disability marked by difficulties in social interaction and communication, as well as unusual interests and behaviours. Sufferers are prone to lash out when they become confused or feel uncomfortable, which makes it difficult for them to form friendships. Dogs working with autistic children need to be super patient and calm.

Step forward the Labernese. A cross between two exceptionally loyal and intelligent companions, the Labrador and the Bernese Mountain Dog, the Labernese has already proved to be a great service dog for the blind and hearing impaired. But it is also demonstrating precisely the right character traits for helping children with autism. As Eric St Pierre, CEO of the foundation explains: 'These dogs have to be patient. They have to remain happy even if the kids are pulling their ears or their fur. They have to forgive a lot.'

Enhancing the natural patience, calm demeanour and loyalty of these dogs is done through training, specifically through play. The next step is to teach the dog, using food treats and plenty of positive reinforcement,

to go to a child who is having an outburst or difficult episode.

Research conducted by MIRA seven years ago indicated that the presence of dogs dramatically lowered the levels of cortisol, the stress hormone, in the 42 children who took part in the study. Less stress meant an overall improvement in the child's development and the atmosphere within the family as a whole. The findings seemed to suggest that with a faithful dog by their side autistic children would be able to interact more and to venture into the kind of unfamiliar situations that would otherwise cause distress and confusion.

This certainly seems to be the case in one household. Fifteen-year-old Marc-Antoine was diagnosed with autism at a young age. Now that his Labernese service dog Tartin is helping him connect more with his surroundings, there have been huge changes in his behaviour. Marc-Antoine used to sleep erratically, but troubled nights have become a thing of the past since Tartin started sleeping in his room. Physical contact with the dog – stroking – provides reassurance and comfort. Sylvie, Marc-Antoine's mother explains: 'When I feel that Marc-Antoine is getting anxious and there is a risk he might have a fit, I ask Tartin to lie down. Then Marc-Antoine lies down too, puts his head on Tartin's belly and listens to his heartbeats. This calms him almost instantly.'

Labernese dogs trained at the MIRA Foundation (*top*) like Tartin (*above*) show the virtues of their breeding – calmness, patience, tolerance of rough handling – which makes them so valuable as stress-lowering companions to children with autism.

3

Aiding
Disability

Aiding Disability

'We interpret Labradors as being intelligent, because for the last 200 years we have selectively bred them to have an enhanced ability or willingness to do things for us.' BRUCE FOGLE, CANINE EXPERT

Like many assistance dog associations, the Japanese Guide Dog Association mainly prefers Labradors for guiding, and raises its own dogs at its Kanagawa Training Centre.

For those who are disabled, small setbacks and irritations can be very disheartening. If you are in a wheelchair and you drop something, you have no choice but to ask someone to retrieve it for you, or do without it. Having to rely on other people for this kind of basic help only serves to emphasize your lack of freedom. Now imagine how much difference it would make to your life to have a dog who is eager to carry out such tasks for you.

Today assistance dogs around the world help people with many different disabilities lead independent lives: there are guide dogs for the blind, hearing dogs for the deaf and service dogs for those with mobility problems. Yet, time and again, those who are aided by dogs say that what they value as much as the practical help is the round-the-clock companionship and love. Assistance dogs aren't simply helpmates, they're soulmates, too.

PICK OF THE BUNCH

Although many different breeds make successful assistance dogs, Labradors and Golden Retrievers are far and away in the majority. Smart,adaptable, good at dealing with stress and natural people-pleasers, it's easy to see why.

Many organizations breed their own pups for assistance training. Even so, not every dog will have what it takes. To make the grade, puppies must display confidence, sociability and willingness to work – an all-round balanced temperament.

REINFORCING THE POSITIVE

By the time assistance dogs are fully trained, they will understand and respond to 40 to 50 different commands. Training is based entirely around positive reinforcement: ignoring the dog when he does not perform correctly and praising and rewarding him when he does. It's all about making learning a game that the dog wants to play. Once that happens, the dog will be motivated to work because it makes him happy.

What is really amazing, however, is that many assistance dogs are able to adapt their training to new circumstances once they have built up a strong rapport with their human partners. This ability to learn as they go along is truly extraordinary.

STAYING FOCUSED

Assistance dogs of all types don't just help their owners in the relative tranquility of the home setting. They must also venture out into busy city streets and other public environments where there are many potential distractions. How do these dogs stay focused on the job at hand?

Studies have shown that high levels of docosahexaenoic acid or DHA in puppyhood contribute to a dog's learning capabilities and can determine how successful it will be as a future guide or companion. Doctor Karen Overall, specialist in canine behaviour, explains: 'DHA is a polyunsaturated fatty acid that is essential for good neuronal development – for the development of good brain tissue. Without it, puppies don't make tight neuronal connections, which makes them more reactive, less attentive and less able to learn.'

Labradors are favoured at the Kanagawa Training Centre partly for their size – a build that is easy for most people to walk with – but also because of their happy, friendly temperament.

'Doors, subway seats, crossings – Axis finds everything on his own. He also helps me meet people. So many come up to me and say how beautiful he is and ask if they can touch him. That gives me the chance to start speaking with them.' MARIE-LAURE ABORNO

BROAD HORIZONS

French guide dog Axis, a border collie, gives his owner Marie-Laure Aborno the freedom to live a full life.

Assistance dogs enhance the lives of their owners by enabling everyday routines to be performed smoothly and safely. But their companionship can be even more transformative, leading those with disabilities to consider whole new opportunities and possibilities for themselves.

Marie-Laure Aborno is 30 years old and has been blind since birth. As is the case with many people who suffer from visual impairment, she had resigned herself to the prospect of depending on others for the rest of her life. But when she was given a guide dog, everything changed for the better. She and her present dog Axis, a Border Collie, have been a team for four years.

Axis is one of over 700 dogs trained by the French Guide Dog Association. His breed makes him particularly suited to this kind of work. As canine eye expert Christine Heinrich explains, this is partly due to anatomical structure: 'Border Collies have much better peripheral vision than that of a little Pug, for example. In the Pug, the head is short and round and the eyes are directed straight ahead, whereas in the Border Collie, with its long nose, the eyes are very divergent, giving a large peripheral visual field.' It is the extent of the dog's peripheral vision that makes it able to spot every last detail and thus anticipate dangers.

Life before having a guide dog was difficult for Marie-Laure. 'In those days I was tired all the time. I even had difficulty getting up in the morning. And when I'm tired, I bump into everything,' she says. By smoothing her path, the dog has made a huge difference to her ability to move from place to place. 'With Axis, I'm relaxed because I don't have to be careful all the time. I know he will protect me from every obstacle. He knows all my routes by heart. If we are in the street or the subway, if there are many people around, he will slalom between them. I used to be much clumsier with the cane. I'm much quicker with Axis.'

With Axis by her side, Marie-Laure not only has mobility, she is able to follow two cherished dreams. The boost in her confidence and independence helped her pursue her career in physiotherapy. 'I always wanted to work to have social recognition,' she says. She also set herself the goal of running marathons and has now competed in five races thanks, in part, to her canine helpmate.

Like many such organizations, the French Guide Dog Association strives to ensure that the temperaments of potential owners and dogs are well-matched. As Mark, a trainer with the association, explains: 'Marie-Laure and Axis are a very good team. She needed a willing and dynamic personality to match hers. We're very happy they work so well together.'

Opal with Satoru Tawada (*left*) and in training (*right*), leading a student across a busy road.

'Dogs' eyes are not suited to reading a book or a newspaper, but they're much superior to people in detecting distant or moving objects. In addition, they check what they see with their nose. Their particular ability is to find their way using both eyes and nose.'

SATORU TAWADA, GENERAL MANAGER AND TRAINER, JGDA

Teacher Training

Labradors Opal and Hotaru use sight and smell to navigate as they learn to be a working guide dog.

The Kanagawa Training Centre, operated by the Japanese Guide Dog Association (JGDA), is one of the largest facilities in the country for raising guide dogs for the blind. It's also home to Japan's first-ever school for guide dog trainers. The course takes three years and both dogs and would-be trainers learn together. Throughout this time, students work with a number of dogs so that they don't become too attached to one animal.

Opal and Hotaru are two of the dogs helping to train future trainers. They're both Labradors. Like many such organizations, the centre mainly favours this particular breed and raises their own dogs on site. Satoru Tawada, general manager and trainer at JGDA, explains that the Lab's build – not too big, not too small – makes it easy and comfortable for people to walk with them. But it's also a question of character and appeal. 'These dogs love people and they're always smiling. Their lovely faces make people feel happy.'

Opal is in the first phase of her training, learning to obey simple commands while walking confidently with her handler along roads and across pedestrian crossings. In the assessment of Erio Sawatri, the student who is currently working with Opal, the dog needs a little more practice. 'She's got to be more accurate. She has to remember and perform what she is expected to do during walk training. I think it will take one more month until she masters all that.'

Hotaru, on the other hand, is approaching his final challenge before he becomes a working guide dog. To pass the test, he will have to lead a blindfolded student, with whom he is not familiar, safely along a specific public route.

According to Satoru Tawada, guide dogs need to master the navigation of three key elements: corners, steps and obstacles. 'Dogs have a huge responsibility to tell their owners where the corners and steps are and also to avoid any obstacles safely.' To do this, dogs not only use their sight, they also employ their remarkable sense of smell as a direction-finder. Training a guide dog entails reinforcing the dog's natural inclination to stop at corners, where they can gain a wider view of their surroundings and sniff out changes in the wind.

An important part of training is working in conditions of low light, and dogs are particularly suited for this. Christine Heinrich, a canine eye expert, says that in addition to their big peripheral visual field, dogs see almost as well in low light as in bright. 'In dim lighting conditions, dogs are able to see objects at a light threshold six times below that which a human would require.'

Currently, there are about a thousand guide dogs in Japan. Opal and Hotaru are not only helping to teach the next generation of guide dog trainers, but their skills will also ensure the safety and independence of their future owners.

ACTIVE DUTY

Injured US soldier Jason Morgan's black Labrador, Napal, has transformed his life, physically and emotionally.

In 1999 Jason Morgan, a member of a special operations unit, was returning from a successful counter-narcotics mission in the middle of the South American jungle when his vehicle was ambushed. The attack, which put him in coma for six weeks and left him paralyzed, spelled the end of his military career. 'I had to wear a full body brace,' says Jason. 'I couldn't dress myself. I couldn't even turn over in bed. My biggest goal was to get my independence back.' For someone who was used to parachuting out of airplanes on active duty, being confined to a wheelchair was exceptionally tough, and it took several years before he could even begin come to terms with the extent of his injuries. But it's only since the arrival of his service dog, Napal, that he has truly come back to life.

Napal, a black Labrador, is one of over 3,000 dogs trained by Canine Companions for Independence since their founding in 1975 (*see* page 43) to assist disabled children and adults. In recent years hundreds have been allocated to veterans returning to the United States from combat zones all over the world. Dogs like Napal undergo two years of professional training before they are ready to be assigned to their handlers. For those who have suddenly lost their mobility, relying on others – canine or otherwise – is a difficult emotional adjustment. To ease the

transition, dogs partnered with veterans have to be particularly well trained and require the minimum of prompting and attention.

And it's not only the dogs that need training. Before Jason could begin to work with his canine companion, he had to take an intensive course to learn how to care for his dog and how to make the most of his unique capabilities. This proved a therapeutic experience in itself. From the moment they were introduced, Napal began to help Jason towards his goal of independence. 'Napal does so much to help me around the house,' says Jason. 'Retrieving objects from the floor. Pulling laundry out of the drier. The things he can do are endless.'

Along with easing Jason's physical struggles, Napal has also brought about a dramatic improvement in his emotional well-being. Before Napal's arrival there were days when Jason wouldn't get out of bed. All this has changed. 'I'm so much more active now. I get up and I do things and I'm much happier for it. Sometimes we just go out and play. The magic that dogs have – they can put a smile on your face whatever you're feeling.' Now, together with Napal, Jason is back on active duty, volunteering at a children's hospital where the dog brings comfort and smiles, and visiting a general ward to reassure patients who are about to have surgery.

'Greater independence is the most important gift you can give to someone in a wheelchair. Napal's changed my whole life and raised my spirits so much. It's been absolutely amazing.' JASON MORGAN

CCI dogs learn over 40 commands and can do a variety of tasks, from guiding to pulling wheelchairs and operating buttons and switches.

'The real magic is when you take these extraordinary dogs that we have bred and trained over the course of two years and we place them with an equally extraordinary person. The people who come to us are looking to take themselves to a new level of independence with a dog's help. Their bodies may not work as well as they would like, but their spirits are soaring.' PAT CALLAHAN, CCI SPOKESPERSON

IT TAKES TWO

Four-legged friends become invaluable
working partners when trained by the
US organization CCI.

Charles Schulz, was the famous US cartoonist and creator of Snoopy, the beagle from his *Peanuts* cartoon strip. In 1975, together with his wife Jean, he founded an amazing organization called Canine Companions for Independence (CCI). Their aim was to provide highly trained assistance dogs to enhance the lives of people with disabilities. CCI is now the largest organization of its kind in the world and has expanded to centres all over the United States from its original base in Santa Rosa, California.

During the course of their two-year training CCI dogs will learn over 40 different commands. By the time of their graduation, they will be able to turn on lights, push buttons, open doors and pull wheelchairs on request. What's more, they will be able to adapt their training to new circumstances as they get to know their handlers and their specific needs.

How do you train such extraordinary dogs? It all starts with the breed. CCI favours Golden Retrievers, Labradors and crosses of the two, breeds that are naturally friendly, well-balanced and that have an instinct to please. Puppies bred for the job are raised by volunteers who nurture and socialize them, teaching them to behave calmly in a variety of situations, from trains and planes to libraries, churches and restaurants.

At fifteen months, the dogs start their training at one of CCI's centres. The general approach is to make it as much fun as possible for the dogs to learn, with plenty of rewards and praise. Building on basic obedience commands, the dogs progress to working around a wheelchair and retrieving on command, before being taught more specific tasks, such as Open Door and Light Switch. 'The dogs have an amazing capacity to learn tasks,' says Keith Reid, a CCI trainer. 'These lessons become routine for them, part of what they are.' During the course of the programme, the dogs are directed to the specific assistance areas that best suit their skills and personality, whether that is as a service dog, hearing dog or a dog destined to work alongside other carers or in institutions. Hearing dogs, for example, have to learn hand signs, as some people with hearing loss cannot vocalize.

The final stage is team training, where the dogs are paired with their future human companions, who learn how to care and look after them, and how to make the best use of what their dogs have been taught to do. It takes two to make a great team. Recipients of these special dogs have to do whatever it takes to make the partnership work.

For those with disabilities, mechanical and technical aids can be invaluable. But nothing beats the love, companionship and sheer joy that these dogs bring to people's lives. As one of CCI's taglines puts it: 'Help is a four-legged word.'

'First, I "hear" through Amos, but second his love and companionship has helped me through some very difficult times. He wants me to be happy and his joy adds sparkle to my life. My life would be empty without him.'

MARIKA REBICSEK

A PERFECT MATCH

Chinese Crested cross breed Amos's devotion
to his owner, Marika Rebicsek, alerts her to
danger as well as helping her live a full life.

Hearing Dogs for Deaf People is a UK charity that trains dogs to alert deaf people to specific sounds at home, at work and in public places. They always look for a good match between potential owners and dogs, which generally comes down to a question of temperament.

Since 1982 the charity has placed more than 1500 hearing dogs and worked with a host of different breeds. One of the most unusual is Amos, who was rescued when he was seven months old and selected by the charity for training.

Amos is a Chinese Crested cross, which is a hairless type of dog. Not only did Amos turn out to have the perfect temperament for his new owner, Marika Rebicsek, his lack of hair meant that she could have a canine helpmate without the risk of her severe pet allergies flaring up. It's a perfect match.

Marika has been profoundly deaf since childhood. After her mother died, she had no one to provide her with the information she needed to live fully. Amos has changed all that for the better. He's both her bridge between the deaf and hearing world and a loving companion who brings joy to her life, helping her to continue to be an active member of the community, teaching sign language at an adult college in Essex. 'He helps me so much when I'm travelling. If I drop something, he comes and shows me with his nose. He's made a massive difference to my life,' says Marika.

Hearing dogs are taught to respond to everyday sounds, such as an alarm clock, doorbell or oven timer, as well as burglar alarms and smoke alarms that signal danger. Once in their new home, they can be trained to recognize more individual noises, such as a baby's cry. Rather than barking, they alert their owner by touch – a paw on the arm of the leg – then lead them to the source of the sound on the command 'What is it?'

One of the wonders of hearing dogs is their ability to extend their training through their own intelligence. Since he has been accompanying Marika to the college where she teaches, Amos has learned to alert her to the bell ringing at the end of the lesson and students like to use him to attract her attention.

On one occasion, Amos was able to prevent a potentially lethal situation when a malfunctioning kettle boiled dry. As Marika explains: 'Amos came up and very emphatically touched me, so I said "What is it?" and he led me to the kitchen. I saw the kettle light was still on, picked it up and nearly dropped it because it was hot. If Amos had not alerted me, it would have caught fire.' This is one of the reasons why this little dog was the winner of the Heroic Hearing Dog of the Year award in 2009.

FREEDOM OF THE CITY

Labrador Tommy uses his intelligence to lead his owner, Blessing Offor, through New York's busy streets.

New York is one of busiest and most exciting cities in the world. Amongst the crowds chasing their dreams in the big city is Blessing Offor, whose ambition is to be a professional musician. Two years ago, Blessing moved to New York from Nashville because there are more opportunities for the type of music he plays.

It's always a challenge to get your first break in a competitive world. But Blessing has an additional obstacle to overcome: he's been blind since the age of five. If, when he arrived in New York, he'd had to find his way around with only a cane to help him it would have been terrifying. But with his Labrador guide dog Tommy in his life, he has the freedom of the city.

Tommy has been trained by a New York charity called Guiding Eyes for the Blind. Unusually, this organization is one of the few guide dog schools in the world which evaluates the temperaments of puppies as young as four weeks old to determine their suitability for training. Kathryn Zubrycki, a trainer with Guiding Eyes, explains that they are looking for dogs that are friendly and energetic, but not overly so. They also have to be willing, confident and able to adapt to new environments without too much fuss. Most of the dogs at Guiding Eyes are Labs and about half the 500 puppies bred at their

Canine Development Center will become working guide dogs like Tommy.

Training starts in quiet areas and then progressively moves to busier ones, with plenty of positive reinforcements and dog treats along the way. Obstacle avoidance is a key part of the dogs' education. They have to be taught to navigate their way around obstructions in a way that is safe for their handler as well as themselves.

Which is where 'intelligent disobedience' comes in. In addition to all their other attributes, guide dogs need good natural instincts. It is this innate sense that enables a guide dog like Tommy to ignore a command where it would put himself and Blessing into danger – if, for example, acting on the command 'Forward' would send them both into the path of an oncoming car. Training a guide dog is all about striking a delicate balance between encouraging a dog's instincts and teaching them to respond to commands.

'Tommy has had a very positive impact on my life,' says Blessing. 'He's made it really easy for me to access public transportation, avoid falling onto train tracks and all that kind of stuff. Travel isn't a big deal with a dog as smart as he is. And his particular brand of cuteness gets me into places I don't think I would otherwise be allowed!'

Traffic and crowds (*top*) are no problem for Blessing Offor as Tommy guides him around the city so that he can pursue his musical ambitions (*left*).

(*Above*) Observing puppies at play gives Guiding Eyes for the Blind vital clues as to their temperament and suitability for training.

'The longer Tommy and I work together, the more he's guided by his instinct of what I feel comfortable with.'

BLESSING OFFOR

Doctor
Dogs

Doctor Dogs

Dogs are good for us in so many ways. Caring for a dog directly enhances physical health, by promoting activity and decreasing stress. Our four-legged friends lift our spirits and improve our mental outlook too, by giving us devoted companionship and by providing the perfect excuse for social interaction. For those with disabilities, assistance dogs are literally a lifeline and the means of accessing the wider world.

A UK charity, Cancer and Bio-detection Dogs, is training dogs to sniff out cancer in humans.

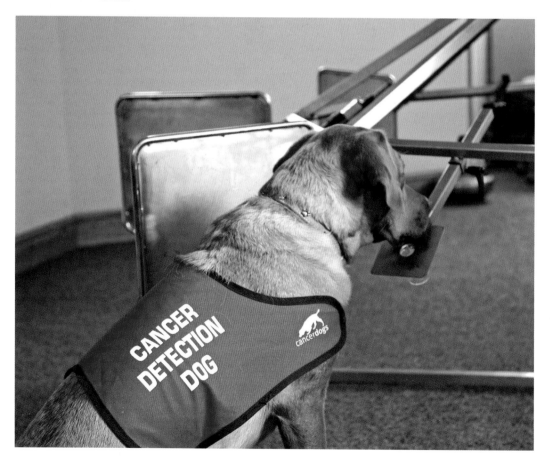

HEALTHY BODY, HAPPY MIND

If you own a dog, you are almost certainly guaranteed better health. This isn't just because of the obvious benefits of daily walks or the fact you are less likely to lie in bed for hours when your pet is urging you to get up and look lively around their empty food bowl. It has been proved by scientific studies that dog owners typically have reduced stress, lower levels of harmful cholesterol, lower blood pressure and are therefore less at risk from heart attacks and strokes.

The good news doesn't end there. Dog owners also enjoy psychological benefits, because dogs are the perfect bridge to meet people socially. Who hasn't taken their dog for a walk in the park and ended up having conversations with total strangers thanks to their canine companion? While dog owners like to swap advice about training and diet, even those without one of their own will often stop to make a fuss over a lovable dog. And as anyone who has ever owned a puppy knows, it is almost impossible to walk more than a few steps without being surrounding by cooing admirers eager to stroke the new arrival.

A WIDER WORLD

Importantly, dogs give those with disabilities new horizons. Isolation and loss of confidence can be a sad side effect of many conditions, but a trained service or assistance dog can provide a whole new lease of life for people who would otherwise be house-bound or dependent on others. By increasing independence and offering comfort and love round the clock, dogs are just what the doctor ordered.

EMERGENCY SERVICES

All dogs have the capacity to improve our lives and general well-being. But some extraordinary canines are so skilled at detecting disease, predicting seizures and other life-threatening episodes that you would think they'd been to medical school.

No one knows for sure how a dog can sense the onset of an epileptic fit, for example, or predict a disastrous drop in a diabetic's blood sugar half an hour before a glucose monitor registers it, or detect a cancer that a scan can't pick up, but their acute sense of smell is thought to play a significant part in their ability to diagnose. Then, too, dogs are observers of human behaviour par excellence, with the ability to spot subtle patterns and signs of which we may not even be aware.

> '*Dogs are very good at exacting information from humans. They have great perceptive ability, which makes them very insightful. Dog owners sometimes think that their dogs are capable of incredibly complicated thought processes, but in fact the dog is just very, very observant.*'
>
> DANIEL MILLS, PROFESSOR OF VETERINARY BEHAVIOURAL MEDICINE, LINCOLN UNIVERSITY

'Max has changed my life and I owe him so much.'
MAUREEN BURNS

EARLY WARNING

Maureen Burns' breast cancer would not have shown up
on a scan – but it was detected by her Collie cross, Max.

*'The Holy Grail in cancer diagnostics is to have a cheap and
simple test that gives you a yes or no answer. That's what we'd
like to see. Maybe by studying dogs in this way we'll get to that.'*
PROFESSOR KAROL SIKORA, CANCER EXPERT

The chances of surviving cancer are greatly
improved if the disease is detected early.
Maureen Burns knows this better than
most. She owes her life to the extraordinary
diagnostic powers of her Collie cross, Max.

In May 2008, the normally energetic Max
became withdrawn and started acting out of
character. 'He wouldn't come and sit next to
me. He wouldn't sit on my lap. He wouldn't
sit near me in the car. He wasn't happy being
with me. And then he'd come up, sniff my
breath and touch my breast.'

Max's unusual behaviour prompted
Maureen to act. When she was examining
herself in the bedroom mirror, she met her
dog's watchful eyes. 'I looked across at Max,
who was on the bed, and that instant I just
knew I had cancer.'

Maureen had found a small lump. On
seeking medical advice, her fears were
confirmed. What's more, she was told that
the cancer she had would not yet show
up on a mammogram or scan. Fortunately,
she has now made a full recovery and Max
is back to his old self. The case supports
growing evidence that some breeds of dog
have the ability to 'sniff out' diseases like
cancer. Certainly Maureen's story comes as
no surprise to the UK charity Cancer and
Bio-detection Dogs. In 2004, the charity,
in association with NHS Buckinghamshire,
conducted a study that proved the dogs

could reliably identify bladder cancer in
human urine samples. The results were
published in the British Medical Journal.

The charity's co-founder and bio-detection
dog trainer Claire Guest puts it down to the
dog's ability to pick volatiles or trace odours,
which certain diseases are understood to
give off. 'They can detect parts per trillion,
a smaller amount of scent than we can
possibly imagine.'

Claire Guest is now training six dogs to
detect other cancers, such as those of the
breast, mouth and prostate, to discover
which have generic odours. The dogs are
given a carousel to sniff. The pots on the
carousel contain urine samples taken from
healthy people, those with cancer, and those
with other illnesses. 'We hope that this work
will lead to developments in the way cancer
is diagnosed. If we can discover, along with
scientists, how a dog detects cancer, then
in the future we could create an electronic
'nose'. Potentially, in ten or fifteen years
time we could go to our doctor's surgery and
give a urine or breath sample that could be
screened for volatiles.'

Dogs have proved themselves to be
lifesavers many times over. But their
incredible ability to detect human disease
may well be their greatest contribution to
our well-being yet.

SPECIAL GIFT

Yorkshire Terrier Poppy's extraordinary natural diagnostic abilities help control her owner Philippa's diabetes, and were developed and honed by the UK charity Cancer and Bio-detection dogs.

Soon after Philippa and her husband Andrew got their Yorkshire Terrier puppy, Poppy, they began to suspect she had a special gift. Now this hidden talent has been honed by training and Philippa's life has changed out of all recognition.

Philippa has suffered from severe Type 1 diabetes since the age of 10. Her body produces no insulin, the hormone that controls blood sugar and is vital for brain and organ function. Despite regular injections and monitoring, some Type 1 diabetics experience drastic swings in blood sugar levels. Low blood sugar can lead to confusion, unconsciousness and fits (called hypoglycaemic attacks or 'hypos'); high blood sugar can result in coma and even death. Unlike many diabetics, Philippa doesn't receive proper warning signals that

her blood sugar is getting dangerously low and in the past has been found unconscious on a number of occasions.

Two years ago, her uncertain health and the stress and worry it was causing her family were getting too much and she retired from her career. 'I could do a great presentation and be very articulate one minute and the next my blood sugar would drop, I'd get confused and it would take me an hour and half to say something simple.' Then Poppy came into her life.

As her husband Andrew explains, Poppy seemed to have an unusual ability: 'I noticed that when Philippa's blood sugar was low Poppy would walk away from her and become agitated. If she was sitting on her lap, she would start to nudge her, as if she was trying to tell her something.'

> '*Poppy has changed my life beyond belief. I feel so much more confident now. I've had people tell me they think my blood sugar's low, but I fully trust Poppy because she doesn't alert me otherwise and that means I can take action.*'
>
> PHILIPPA COPLESTON-WARREN

> '*I don't have to be so anxious and worried now because I know that Poppy is keeping a better eye on Philippa than I or anyone else ever could.*'
>
> ANDREW WARREN

Philippa contacted the UK charity Cancer and Bio-detection Dogs to see if Poppy's instinct could be developed. The charity trains dogs to detect the odour of human disease, including 'hypo-alert' dogs that indicate to their owners when blood sugar levels are abnormal. When sugar levels are high, acids called ketones are released. These have a distinctive pear drop smell that even we humans can recognize. However, despite extensive studies, no one knows exactly how dogs are able to identify when the sugar level is low, but scent, too, is thought to play a large part.

The charity trained Poppy to alter her alert from agitation and withdrawal to yawning and nibbling Philippa's finger. Extraordinarily, Poppy is able to warn Philippa that her blood sugar has risen or fallen half an hour before the same results show up on her glucose monitor. This gives her the time to take preventative action – a tiny bit more insulin if levels are high, or a glass of orange juice if they are dropping. Normal levels of blood sugar are between 5 and 6mmol/L. Poppy sounds the alarm when Philippa's drop to 4.5mmol/L. Thanks to this tiny Yorkie, Philippa has a new sense of independence and control.

Stand By Me

The acute senses of Maybe the Golden Labrador warn her owner Christine Prajanowa of an imminent epileptic seizure and keep her safe during an attack.

Christine and her Golden Labrador Maybe are inseparable. Everywhere Christine goes, everything she does, Maybe is right by her side. But this is not simply a case of canine devotion. Maybe has an important job to do: she's a life-saver, an early warning system and Christine's means of accessing a full and independent life.

Over twenty years ago, Christine, who lives in Waregem, Belgium, was diagnosed with a form of epilepsy that means she suffers from recurrent and sudden seizures, during which she loses consciousness and her whole body becomes stiff. The seizures can happen anywhere and without warning. In the past, she's broken her nose, toes and wrist and dislocated her shoulder as a result. After her diagnosis, her fear of falling in the street was so great she soon stopped going out for walks by herself. Although medication helped control the condition, she had to give up work, give up driving and gradually lost social contact.

All that changed about nine years ago when Christine got in touch with the Hachiko Centre, an organization that trains assistance dogs for people with motor disabilities or those suffering from epilepsy. That was when Maybe came into her life and completely transformed it.

Seizure response dogs are trained to prevent people from falling in dangerous areas and to provide essential help, such as pushing alarm buttons or fetching medication, immediately after a seizure has occurred. When Christine falls, Maybe will run to her desk and pick up her bag of medication, then she will lie down beside her. When she senses the seizure is over, she will start barking really loudly until Christine can sit up. If she's not able to stand, Maybe will fetch the phone.

Caroline Thienpont, trainer at the Hachiko Centre, explains that seizure response dogs are trained to bark after a seizure because sufferers regain their sense of hearing before they are able to see or speak. The sound of their dog barking gives them reassurance that they are not alone and help is at hand.

But Maybe is one of the select few who are able to alert their owner before a seizure even occurs. Half an hour before Christine is going to have a seizure, Maybe will start licking her wrists very intensely so she has time to get into a safe position. The comfort of this advance knowledge has lowered Christine's stress levels considerably, which in turn has made the seizures less frequent. 'Before, I wouldn't go out for walks,' says Christine. 'Now that's possible because Maybe stops me at every crossroad . . . she always gets me safely to the other side. I can't begin to say how much she's changed my life.'

'There's no question that some dogs can tell beforehand that an individual is going to have a seizure. It isn't understood whether they pick up a scent or subtle body language that suggests something is wrong but they detect something.'

BRUCE FOGLE, CANINE EXPERT

ONE IN A MILLION

Bingo the Jack Russell regularly saves his owner's life, by barking a warning when Cole is about to suffer a life-threatening episode.

Like many small boys, nine-year-old Cole Hein is devoted to his dog, a lively little Jack Russell. But Cole's attachment to Bingo is extra special, because ever since she came to live with him at his home in Shilo, Manitoba, she has saved his life many times.

Cole suffers from apnoea, a life-threatening and incurable condition that causes him to retch and stop breathing with little or no warning. He and his twin brother Eric were born three months early and, in common with many premature babies, both suffered from apnoea, which is generally a temporary problem. Unlike his brother, however, Cole did not outgrow the condition.

By the time Cole was four, his mother Mandi was averaging only four hours' sleep a night. Exhausted, and with the whole family living under constant fear that Cole's next attack might be his last, she turned to an unusual source of help: a Canadian charity called National Service Dogs (NSD) that trains dogs to help people with special needs. Her question was whether a dog could be trained to alert her when Cole was having an episode.

NSD had never had a request like this before, but Danielle Forbes, NSD's Executive Director, thought she might be able to help. It would take the right training – and it would take the right dog.

That dog was Bingo. As a former hearing dog, she already had a solid start in training. She had also been raised in a family and was used to children. When she was introduced to Cole and his family, she fitted in from day one. The next challenge was to give her the skills to help Cole.

Unlike most Jack Russells, Bingo is not inclined to bark. This made her the perfect candidate for the job, as she needed to learn to bark only when Cole was in trouble. Using hand signals, and plenty of rewards, Danielle first taught Bingo to bark on command, then she linked the hand signals to a recording of one of Cole's episodes. After weeks of intensive training, Bingo was responding perfectly on cue. All the positive reinforcement meant that Bingo came to associate the sound of retching, which precedes the apnoea, with nice things, like play and dog treats.

The training worked. One night Cole suffered an episode when his parents were asleep and Bingo alerted them by barking excitedly. From then on, the family knew they could trust the little dog one hundred percent, and it has made a difference to all their lives. 'Now when Cole's sick,' says Mandi, 'he doesn't look to me, he looks to her. He knows it's that much better if Bingo's there.'

'Even when dogs are asleep they can pick up sounds inaudible to humans and react to them.'

DAVID MORGAN, CANINE EXPERT

'Bingo is one in a million. It's not the fact that she's a Jack Russell, it's to do with her personality. She was the right dog at the right time for the right family. There are no words to describe how it feels to see a dog we have trained make the difference to a child between life and death.'

DANIELLE FORBES, CO-FOUNDER AND EXECUTIVE DIRECTOR, NATIONAL SERVICE DOGS.

5

Sixth
Sense?

Sixth Sense?

The sensitive canine nose, like that of the American Foxhound (*left*) can detect pheromones emitted by humans and so may be able to 'smell' our moods. Some breeds, like the American Staffordshire Terrier (*right*), are particularly anxious to please and so seem sensitive their owners emotions.

Dogs are full of surprises. As many dog owners will testify, sometimes it's as if our pets can read our minds, anticipating our next move or sensing the way we are feeling. Whether we're happy or out of sorts, dogs somehow seem to know and respond accordingly, joining in the excitement, or coming to offer us their special brand of comfort.

In a number of extraordinary cases, however, the empathetic powers of dogs have strayed into the realm of the truly inexplicable. Dogs that can accurately predict seismic activity, the approach of stormy weather – even death – seem to possess an uncanny sixth sense.

SUPER SENSES

Do dogs really possess a sixth sense? Or is it the case that their incredible sensory awareness, particularly in terms of hearing and smell, gives them access to information that is far beyond our ken? It is known, for example, that dogs can smell bitches in heat miles away. The possession of faculties as acute as that may cast light on the many cases where dogs are reported to have anticipated their owners' arrival home many minutes before they've reached the front door.

Scientists have long debated the theory that dogs can actually smell our moods. When we experience strong emotional reactions like fear, we produce pheromones. It appears that dogs can pick up on these cues as our bodies emit these changes of scent.

BODY LANGUAGE

All dogs are fluent in one particular language: body language. They're very good at picking up predictable patterns of behaviour. This often shows up during training. If you teach your dog to 'Sit' on command and generally follow that up with the instruction 'Shake', you may well find that after you tell your dog to 'Sit' it will offer you its paw without being asked to.

According to Daniel Mills, Professor of Veterinary Behavioural Medicine at Lincoln University, dogs can even understand the rudiments of grammar. 'Dogs can distinguish between 'sit' and 'sat', for example. Research from Austria has also shown that they acknowledge equity. If they get a biscuit for doing a job well, that is fine. But if they see another dog get two biscuits for doing the same job, they don't like it.'

BRAIN WAVES

In our daily life, we humans rely heavily on the frontal lobe of our brains, the area associated with planning and problem-solving. Dogs, on the other hand, are much more attuned to the area of the brain that deals with emotions. The limbic system, as it is known, includes the hypothalamus, the hippocampus and the amygdala, and it is not only the seat of emotional feeling, it also has a great deal to do with memory. This may explain why dogs are both good at picking up the emotions we display and learning patterns of human behaviour.

'Dogs chiefly use the emotional part of their brain. The result is they read us extraordinary well, probably better than we read other people. They're familiar with interpreting our body language and the changes in the way we smell, and they pick up our emotional states that way.'
BRUCE FOGLE, CANINE EXPERT

FELLOW FEELING

Research at the University of Otago in New
Zealand is beginning to show that dogs
really do sense our emotions.

One of the central aspects of our enduring relationship with dogs is the value we place on their love and companionship. At times, the closeness of this bond has naturally led us to believe that our dogs can sense what we are feeling. Particularly when we're upset or out of sorts, those warm doggy eyes looking up at us seem to be full of empathy. But are we anthropomorphizing our pets, or is there any truth in it?

In a fifteen-month-long study, Associate Professor Ted Ruffman at the University of Otago, Dunedin, New Zealand, set out to uncover whether dogs really can read human emotions. Together with a team of students, he has put 58 dogs of all shapes, sizes and breeds through a series of tests. As Professor Ruffman explains: 'Dog owners are pretty much uniformly agreed that their dogs understand them. This is plausible because humans have been breeding dogs for thousands of years, selecting certain qualities that they like. So I thought, OK, let's look at this scientifically.'

Previous research exploring the neurological effects of interactions between humans and dogs have established that the levels of hormones associated with elation are raised in both species during pleasurable encounters between them, while levels of stress hormones decrease. The question for Professor Ruffman and his team was whether the release of these happy chemicals in our brains deludes us into thinking that our dogs understand our feelings.

During the study, the dogs were set certain tasks, all designed to determine how they might react if they did understand human emotions. In a 'social referencing' task, a toy robot was set up to emerge from a box in front of the dog. At the sight of the robot, researcher Min Hooi Yong would assume either a happy expression or a fearful one. In another experiment, the dog was given a treat. Then Min would give the command 'Leave' – in a happy voice, an angry voice or a voice of disgust – before leaving the room for a minute. In yet another test, she would play the sound of a baby crying or babbling happily while half-hidden behind a barrier.

So far the experiments have yielded some interesting results. Professor Ruffman has found that the dogs were more likely to approach the toy robot if the researcher reacted happily towards it, rather than fearfully. The dogs were also more likely to leave the food treat for longer if the command had been given in an angry voice. The sound of crying provoked a different response in the dogs than the sound of babbling. When they listened to the crying, they cocked their heads more, signaling greater interest. 'In a nutshell, these results are consistent with the idea that dogs do understand human emotional expression in some sense,' says Professor Ruffman.

'We know that dogs have been man's best friend for many years now and owners in the past have bred dogs for particular traits, one of which is social companionship. Dogs are tuned into human emotion more than we give them credit for.'

MIN HOOI YONG, RESEARCHER AT THE
UNIVERSITY OF OTAGO

'If my partner and I are having a bit of a set-to, the dog will come between us, his ears will go back and he'll want a pat or a cuddle. The interesting thing is that it often works. You get distracted and forget what the argument was about in the first place.'

SALLY SHAW, DOG OWNER
RESEARCH VOLUNTEER

Dogs at the University of Otago were set tasks and exposed to a variety of situations – such as being presented with a toy robot – to gauge their reactions when people were also present and displaying different emotions.

'Scamp ended up becoming a nursing-home resident, giving lots of attention, lots of love. He spent so much time here with these people . . . I think he knew, he had a sense that something was not right.'

DEIRDRE, SCAMP'S FORMER OWNER

SAYING GOODBYE

Miniature Schnauzer Scamp's incredible sensitivity to the residents of a US nursing home seems to make him aware when they are nearing the end of their days.

Can dogs predict the future? Can they tell, for example, when someone is about to die? Sceptics would say that's impossible, but the owners of The Pines nursing home in Canton, Ohio have plenty of evidence to suggest otherwise.

In the six years since Scamp, a Miniature Schnauzer, has been living at the home, he has predicted no fewer than 40 deaths, which is half of those that have occurred there during that period. The numbers would seem to suggest this is perhaps more than sheer coincidence.

When Deirdre, a former nurse, first brought Scamp to the home, she gave him a toy, a little stuffed cow, which he carried with him everywhere, enjoying the love and the attention bestowed on him by the residents. Soon she started to spot the toy at certain bedsides, indicating where the dog was spending more of his time. Then she noticed that when someone was passing away, the dog would come up the hall barking.

Adeline Baker, who runs the home and now looks after Scamp, also began to see a pattern emerging. 'It seemed like every time someone was not doing well, Scamp would get more and more stressed out. Or we would find his toy in the bed of someone who was dying. It was like he was making himself known and visiting people when they were passing away.'

Ever since Scamp has repeatedly barked and paced around the beds of dying residents, refusing to leave their rooms in their final hours. His 'premonition' skills have become something of a warning system at the nursing home. 'He barks, gets agitated and scratches at the doors of people who are not doing well. If we don't pick up on it, he comes and barks at us until we get up and look.'

Experts have speculated how dogs like Scamp are seemingly able to make such accurate prognoses. Explanations range from dogs simply mimicking human behaviour to their incredible sense of smell. It is sometimes argued, for example, that they may be able to pick up the scent of certain chemicals released by humans as their vital organs begin to deteriorate.

For whatever reason, Scamp's incredible ability has provided an element of comfort to friends and families, who value the time he buys them to say their cherished goodbyes to their loved ones. Angie, a volunteer at The Pines, used to come to the nursing home every day to look after one of the residents, Phyllis, her friend of 55 years. 'Before Phyllis passed away, Scamp kept coming in her room. The second day, when she wasn't responding at all, he kept coming in the room and pawing me and I knew something was going to happen.'

TALK TO ME

In Hungary, researchers at the University of Budapest are discovering meaning in the sound of a dog's bark.

Barking is one of a dog's most fundamental characteristics, yet we know relatively little about it. Now, a groundbreaking study in this formerly neglected area of research has been conducted by behavioural biologist Peter Pongracz of Eötvös Loránd University, Budapest. Over the course of ten years, Peter has explored a number of aspects of canine communication, ranging from whether a dog can distinguish between the meaning of different growls to whether dogs can judge size through the pitch of a bark, and in the process uncovered fascinating new results that demonstrate just how complex dog communication really is.

Dogs have their own personality traits and these can be clearly distinguished by how they react to a bark. In the 'Habituation/ Dishabituation Bark Experiment' four recorded barking samples were played to the dogs being studied. The first three samples were barks from a dog tied to a tree and left alone by its owner; the fourth was a bark from a different dog. Stoke, a bulldog, and Chilli, a Hungarian Mudi, took part in the experiment to see if they would react with more interest to the fourth bark. The more outgoing Stoke did respond with a bark.

'The Bone is Mine Experiment' was devised by Peter to assess whether dogs react to growls according to context. 'We wondered if dogs can understand exactly what another dog is growling about,' he says. Recordings of three different growls were used: playful growls, growls made at the advance of a threatening stranger, and food-guarding growls. The dogs in the study were presented with a delicious bone and the different growls were played. When a food-guarding growl was played to Stoke he backed away from the bone. When the playful growl was played, even timid Chilli had no hesitation taking the bone.

To explore whether dogs can gauge size from a bark or a growl, the images of two dogs, one larger than the other, were projected on a screen. When Stoke came into the room and the sound of a bark was played, he immediately fixed on the image of the dog that corresponded in size and didn't even glance at the other dog picture.

Dogs can evidently understand and communicate with each other in exceedingly complex ways, if the issues addressed by Peter Pongracz's research are anything to go by. Doctor Karen Overall, canine expert, agrees: 'If you walk through a kennel of rescue dogs, you'll hear high-pitched distress barks, which are very different from the way your dog will bark at home when someone comes to the door. They're sending different messages. If people would do more sonographic work on dogs and begin to map these patterns, I think we could find that dogs do have a sort of vocal language. How much it's like speech, we'll have to wait and see, but I'm at the point where I wouldn't be surprised about anything.'

Chilli (*top and bottom*) and Stoke (*middle*) were participants in a number of experiments at Eötvös Loránd University, Budapest.

'Imagine a simple scenario. You are at home with your dog and another dog starts to bark outside. Your dog doesn't react at all. The next time, the same dog starts to bark again and your dog jumps up and runs to the fence, looking for something. This tells you dogs can clearly hear differences in the barks of other dogs.'

PETER PONGRACZ

To the
Rescue

To the Rescue

'If you're going to train a dog to track people, it's important to choose your samples carefully. If you only ever use samples from one person, for instance, the dog may not make the leap to understand that it is looking for any potential member of the same species, rather than a particular individual.'

DANIEL MILLS, PROFESSOR OF VETERINARY BEHAVIOURAL MEDICINE, LINCOLN UNIVERSITY

When natural disasters strike, it's a race against the clock to locate survivors before it's too late. Victims of devastating earthquakes or avalanches, buried under tons of rubble or snow, need to be located fast if they are to stand a chance of getting out alive and relatively unscathed. The same is true for those who find themselves at sea in serious trouble, either by underestimating their own prowess and stamina, or who are beset by sudden and adverse conditions they haven't anticipated.

Dogs have long played a role in rescuing people from whatever misfortunes befall them. The benign, thick-coated St Bernard, a reviving mini-keg of brandy tied round its neck, is a breed whose efforts on behalf of travellers come to grief in the Alpine regions of Europe have passed into legend.

Only relatively recently have dogs become an essential part of professionally trained international rescue teams, ready to fly out at a moment's notice to trouble spots round the world. Many people today owe their lives to the extraordinary qualities of these canine Samaritans.

International Rescue dog Eros is put through his paces by his handler, Hidehiro Murase (*see* page 80). Regular training is essential to keep up these specialized skills.

CRY FOR HELP

Despite all the sophisticated technology we have at our command today, such as thermal-imaging equipment, nothing beats a dog's nose when it comes to finding people who are in urgent need of rescue – and finding them fast. All dogs have exceptional senses of smell, but rescue dogs have something more – the ability to differentiate between all the other heady odours presented to their nostrils at a disaster site and hone in on the one that will make the difference between a victim surviving and perishing. Certain breeds of dog are particularly good at what is known as 'air scenting' which allows the animal to locate a human scent from more than a quarter of a mile away.

It's all down to a combination of nature and nurture. Great rescue dogs often come from breeds and stock that exhibit superior olfactory powers. But training is also the key to ensure their spectacular sensory abilities are kept up to the mark.

COVERING THE GROUND

Where dogs also have the edge on human rescuers is in their capacity to tackle very inhospitable terrain or conditions at great speed, covering vast areas in a fraction of the time it would take their handlers. Disaster sites, whatever their nature, present very difficult conditions – ground that might be subject to on-going tremors, unsteady piles of rubble that may collapse at any moment or cold, windy conditions at high altitudes.

To do their job, these dogs need all their innate qualities of agility and stamina, traits that can also be enhanced by routine work-outs and training. As is the case with all the services dogs who perform for our benefit, rescue work ultimately depends on the dog's desire to please its handler and its joy in exercising its skills. It may be a matter of life or death, but to a rescue dog, it's all in a day's play.

MAKING A SPLASH

The bravery, strength and agile swimming skills of Golden Retriever Zoe makes her one of the stars of the Italian School of Water Rescue Dogs.

During the peak summer season the beautiful Italian coastline and lakes are teeming with bathers and boaters enjoying the water and warm sunshine. To keep the holidaymakers safe lifeguards are on patrol. Among them is a dog called Zoe. Zoe can swim over 2km, jump out of a helicopter from a height of 5m into the water and pull dinghies to shore with her teeth. She has saved many lives and is one of the best in the business.

Zoe is a graduate of the Italian School of Water Rescue Dogs, set up by former emergency services volunteer Ferrucio Pilenga. Full training takes three years and involves intensive swimming and distance training as well as specific exercises. Dogs have to be able to swim and simultaneously drag a human for up to an hour in rough waters, or support a victim while their handlers perform first-aid procedures such as mouth-to-mouth resuscitation. After the water training is completed the dogs are then taught to jump from hovering helicopters, which first means getting them accustomed to the noise and choppy waters created by high rotor speeds. 'The most important thing,' says Renato Cumia, Zoe's handler, 'is that they have to be happy to work. It's a game for them.'

Studies have suggested that dogs are one of the few non-aquatic mammals that can hold their breath. This helps them perform even if their heads are immersed by protecting the larynx from the entry of water into their lungs. While most dogs can swim – hence the term 'doggy paddle' – some take to the water much more happily than others. These include working dogs such as Labradors and Golden Retrievers, who may have to venture into water to fetch game, along with Newfoundlands, which were originally bred to work with fishermen.

Newfoundlands, in particular, are ideal for water rescue work. Their natural swimming stroke is more like breaststroke than doggy paddle and they have thick waterproof coats that protect them from the cold, along with slightly webbed feet that maximize thrust. Their big lung capacity helps them swim long distances, while their large skeletons give them the strength and power to resist strong tides. Large dogs can have a bite force double that of a human's, so they can handle the pressure required to drag a boat.

Three years ago, while they were on vacation, Zoe and her handler Renato rescued two fishermen whose boat had capsized. Incredibly, Zoe managed to drag the two men and the boat safely to shore using her teeth. 'They were astonished, but she did it because she was trained to do it,' says Renato.

Above Zoe sets out for a helicopter rescue. *Below* Newfoundland Water Rescue dog Vera sets out for a training exercise with her teammates.

CANI SALVATAGGIO ★ PROTEZIONE CIVILE

 # ON SHAKY GROUND

Search and rescue dogs in New Zealand have to be adaptable, working in extreme conditions, from snow-capped mountains to the rubble of earthquake-shattered skyscrapers.

New Zealand is famous for the beauty and variety of its landscape, which includes snow-capped mountain ranges, unspoilt wilderness and stunning coastlines. Yet as its nickname, 'The Shaky Islands', implies, the country's location on a number of fault lines has made it prone to earthquakes, avalanches and landslides.

When disaster strikes, speed is of the essence to find people who may be trapped under a collapsed building or buried in snow. It is the dog's ability to search a wide area fast and pinpoint the location of a missing person using its extraordinary sense of smell that makes it ideal for such rescue work.

New Zealand Urban Search and Rescue (USAR) and Land Search and Rescue (LandSAR) consist of teams of dogs and their handlers, trained to operate in urban and remote locations. Regular training sessions keep the dogs fit and eager to work.

Although dogs are naturally agile, practice keeps them up to speed. As Brendon Irwin, head of operations USAR, explains: 'We do have to put quite a bit of work into their agility. We basically get bits of junk, piles of

> '*If a team of rescue workers searched an average-sized rubble pile – say 20m by 20m by 3m high – it might take anywhere from two to five hours to find anyone trapped underneath. A dog will search the same area in two to five minutes.*'
>
> BRENDON IRWIN, HEAD OF OPERATIONS, USAR

Dogs from New Zealand's Land Search and Rescue are trained to work in snowy terrain.

old pallets, empty drums and heap them up to get the dogs comfortable with their feet being unsteady.'

In the worst-case scenario, dogs may be required to climb over obstacles as large as collapsed 20-storey buildings. While covering such unstable ground as fast as they can, they must hone in on a scent they have never smelled before and locate its source without hurting themselves. Brendon explains: 'Even though someone may be trapped under concrete, there's usually enough scent flow coming up for the dogs to detect it. It works a bit like smoke coming up a chimney.'

Away from urban areas, rescue dogs have to cope with similarly difficult terrain, such as steep cliff sides and snowy mountains prone to avalanches. Dave Krehic, LandSAR handler, and his dog Stig have worked all over New Zealand and regularly participate in training exercises to increase their performance. Thanks to Stig's agility and his amazing ability to bounce down cliffs and clamber round narrow edges, they can clear an area in half an hour, compared to the whole day it would take human rescuers working on their own.

Millie, a black Labrador, is another hard-working LandSAR dog used to demanding and hazardous conditions. Specialist avalanche training introduces dogs like her to high wind speeds that can make scent even more difficult to detect. Millie's handler Brendan Kearns is full of admiration for the breed's abilities: 'Avalanches generally result in large broken blocks of snow. We find the black Labradors are really good at climbing over the blocks. They're strong, agile and can deal with the terrain.'

'For me, working with Lola is a luxury. When you feel destroyed and all you want to do is rest, she will come and give you a kiss or ask to play. Dogs are very perceptive that way.'

CRISTIAN KUPERBANK,
HEAD OF UNRS

Dogs from Argentina's UNRS rescue organisation (like Lola, seen above with her handler Cristian) are trained to find people hidden in locations that are a realistic approximation to disaster zones.

LOST AND FOUND

Earthquake victims in Haiti and Chile owe their survival to Lola, a Labrador from Argentina, and the training given by her handler Cristian Kuperbank.

On the 12th January 2010 a massive earthquake struck Haiti, devastating the capital Port-au-Prince and surrounding areas. In the immediate aftermath, search and rescue teams arrived from all over the world in a joint mission to hunt for survivors buried under the rubble. Among them was Lola, a remarkable brown Labrador. Today nine victims of the quake owe their lives to her extraordinary abilities.

Labradors like Lola make superb search and rescue dogs. Their dense body frame, built for strength and agility, enables them to move at speed over irregular or uneven surfaces, while their superior sense of smell means they can sniff out humans at great distances. Their innate friendliness is also a vital factor, as during a mission these dogs may be called upon to cooperate with someone other than their handler. On a typical search, Lola can cover an area of as much as 3 million square metres/3.5 million square yards in just a few days, much faster than any human could.

Lola's handler, Cristian Kuperbank, is head of Unidad Canina de Rescate y Salvamento Ong K9 Ezeiza Argentina (UNRS), an organization based in Buenos Aires. His job is to make sure that Lola and the other UNRS dogs remain focused on the job at hand, ready to be deployed at a moment's notice. Twice a month he and his team train their dogs by getting them to find people hiding in various locations. A key element of Lola's training is to improve her ability to pick up the scent of a person she's never met amongst the thousands of other odours bombarding her nostrils. 'We intervene in situations where we don't have the victim's clothing and where there are countless victims,' says Cristian.

The basis of training is to make it a game. Completing a task successfully wins the dog a 'biter', a stuffed cushion with a handle, and the chance to play with it. Cristian explains: 'At the beginning, the exercises are basic and the dog sees where the person hides. Then we increase the level of difficulty, to encourage the dog to use its most valuable sense, its nose.'

But there's more. Lola is trained not only to locate missing persons but also to indicate whether they are alive or dead. 'When Lola finds a living person she has to bark and when she finds a dead person she has to scratch,' says Cristian. 'When the buried person is alive and I throw Lola her toy, she plays with it. But when she finds a corpse and I reward her in the same way, she takes it by the handle and carries it away delicately.'

Following Lola's success in the aftermath of both the Haitian and Chilean earthquakes, she now has a new mission. She's been asked by the Buenos Aires police force to help out in a missing person's case.

A NOSE FOR TROUBLE

International Rescue Dog Eros, a German
Shepherd from Japan, has such a highly
developed locating ability that he can search
independently of his handler, Hidehiro Murase.

All dogs have powerful senses of smell.
But in some, like seven-year-old German
Shepherd Eros, that natural ability is
incredibly highly developed.

Eros and his handler, Hidehiro Murase,
are the only mission-readiness-tested (MRT)
rescue dog team in Japan, as certified by
the International Rescue Dog Organization
(IRO) based in Salzburg, Austria. This means
that their services can be called upon in the
event of a disaster happening anywhere in
the world.

In 2009, Eros and Hidehiro assisted in the
aftermath of the earthquake that struck the
Indonesian island of Sumatra. Conditions
were extremely difficult, as Hidehiro recalls:
'The temperature was really high and moving
between the sites was hard. Transport was
badly affected. In those conditions Eros
had to keep up the fitness he gained from
everyday training.' Battling temperatures in
excess of 36°C, as well as monsoon rains,
the dog used his remarkable detection
abilities to search for potential survivors
trapped under collapsed buildings.

What is extraordinary about Eros is that
his nose is so good he is able to search
independently, devising his own plan of
action to locate victims. 'He was born with
a talent, an excellent sense of smell,' says
Hidehiro, 'and he uses it with his thinking.
He works with a human-like rational mind.'

Daisaku Sato, spokesperson with the
Rescue Dog Trainers Association, to which
Hidehiro belongs, explains that dogs don't
just rely on smell to find people. 'Intelligent
dogs will look around and feel the air of the
site, fully using all their senses to locate the
source of the smell.'

All IRO-certified dogs have to undergo
regular training sessions to ensure their
skills remain up to scratch. The only training
course in Japan that meets the approved
standard for such training is at Fujimi in
Kanagawa province. It's fiendishly difficult.
Designed to simulate a real rubble-search
environment as closely as possible, it is
situated in a densely forested area. The air
here carries many different smells that could
prove distracting for all but the keenest of
noses. Fallen trees, underground drainage
pipes, tyres and simulated smoke makes the
challenge even greater.

On the day, Eros completes the rubble
search with flying colours, finding both
people who were hiding there. Which is only
what you would expect from a dog that came
fourth in the 2009 IRO world championships.
The test over, he is once again on stand-by
for disaster rescue work.

Looking back at archive photos taken
when Eros was working in Sumatra after
the earthquake, Hidehiro is convinced the
dog can tell the difference between a real
site and a training exercise. 'I can definitely
see from his face that he is aware this is
a real rescue. I can tell that he knows that
it is different from everyday training. He
doesn't speak words, but between us we can
understand each other well enough.'

'If we go to a rescue site, I am confident that he can find trapped people there. If the site is harder to search, he will tackle it with more ability. I have no doubt in him.'
HIDEHIRO MURASE, RESCUE DOG TRAINERS ASSOCIATION

SLIPPERY SLOPE

Rescuing skiers trapped under snow in Aspen Highlands, Colorado, is a serious game for black Labrador Kaya.

The snow-covered peaks of Aspen Highlands in Colorado are a popular destination throughout the ski season, with thousands of people enjoying the slopes and the challenging backcountry trails. But, as in many such regions, avalanches are not an uncommon occurrence and their devastating power can cost lives.

Ski Patrol Director Mac Smith has been patrolling Aspen Highlands for 38 years. Pre-season snow compaction and the use of explosives to trigger small slides is part of the avalanche control work carried out by him and his team. If, despite such preventative measures, an avalanche does occur, essential backup is provided by a black Labrador called Kaya, one of three dogs specially trained to locate humans trapped under snow. 'The dogs are very instrumental in what we do,' says Mac.

Patrols carry avalanche beacons so they can be located quickly if they get into trouble. Many backcountry skiers do the same, or carry transceivers. For those that don't, the extraordinary scenting powers of dogs like Kaya represent their best chance of surviving an avalanche.

Kaya is a highly trained air-scenting dog, able to detect human scent from more than a quarter of a mile away. She can search a snow burial site of 10,000 square feet/930 square metres in less than 20 minutes, a job it would take a human searcher three to

four hours to complete. If she finds someone buried under the snow, she gives a bark alert and starts digging frantically.

As Kaya's handler Lori Spence explains, speed is of the essence. 'It's best to get the dogs into the area before the scent of all the rescuers comes in. The sooner we can get on that snow pack, the better the chance of survival.' To transport Kaya to a site, Lori will ski there carrying the dog on her shoulders. 'We love to ski with the dogs on our shoulders because it's quick. We don't have to get a snow cat or a snowmobile ready. When they're young we start to train them to jump on our shoulders and stay there while we ski. Once they're up there, they're super-comfortable and they're close to the one they love the most.'

Avalanche rescue dogs endure rigorous training. They need to learn to walk on slippery snow and ice and their eyes need to become accustomed to the blinding white snow. Dan Goddard is a trainer with the Avalanche Rescue Program. 'We start with simple games to engage the dogs' interest. Then we move on through the drills. We call it a game, because that's essentially how the dogs see it. A game with an extreme reward at the end.'

Kaya comes from a long line of field trail dogs. 'It's her instinct to go go go,' says Lori. 'She just wants to be moving all the time. Not all dogs have so much drive as Kaya.'

Previous page Kaya searching in the snow. *Above* Lori Spence, Kaya's handler, makes sure Kaya has fun in between rescue missions. *Below* Kaya and her other team members – golden Labrador Sienna and Australian Shepherd Gus enjoy a moment of relaxation.

Conserve
& Protect

Conserve & Protect

The skills and abilities that make hunting dogs, like these Poitevin hounds, so successful at their task can be put to use in tracking endangered species or saving habitats by sniffing out destructive invaders.

In recent years, environmental issues have come ever more to the forefront, as awareness grows of the great challenges we face if we are to ensure the survival of our planet. All around the world, fragile habitats are threatened by climate change, the encroachment of human settlements, rapid deforestation and a host of other adverse factors. Dogs can't do much to stop illegal logging or reduce carbon emissions. They can't change our wasteful lifestyles. But they are proving surprisingly successful helpmates both in conservation of endangered species and in the fight to protect delicate ecosystems from alien invaders.

Dogs are natural predators, primed to use their senses, particularly their spectacular sense of smell, to track down prey. Now, ironically, these predatory instincts are being harnessed in an attempt to protect and conserve other species, both plant and animal.

These eco-warriors are just doing what comes naturally. But they are doing a job that humans, with their limited sensory powers, couldn't possibly attempt themselves, and operating in conditions that often test their endurance to the maximum.

THE HUNTING INSTINCT

As a direct descendant of the wolf, the dog retains a strong hunting instinct, which is closely related to its instinct for social co-operation. Basic obedience training – teaching dogs to 'Sit', for example – does not do much to satisfy either of these instincts, any more than it provides a good physical work-out, which is something else that dogs crave. On the other hand, training that addresses a dog's innate drive to search for prey, along with its desire to co-operate and please other members of its pack, unleashes the full range of a dog's extraordinary capabilities.

NOSEWORK

As humans we are sight-oriented creatures and much of the information that we process about the world comes in visual form. That's not the case with dogs, whose world is overwhelmingly one of smell. Training that involves 'nosework' is playing to a dog's inherent strengths and is far more interesting for a dog on that account.

REWARD

Many owners train their dogs using food treats as rewards. When it comes to getting a dog to perform a task correctly, however, food is less of an incentive than you might think. Treats are particularly ineffective if the dog isn't hungry.

What's striking about professional dog trainers is how rarely they use food rewards in their teaching. Yet they achieve spectacular results. One of the reasons is because they are training the dog to do something it actively wants to do. Just as people enjoy exercising whatever talents they have to the full, so do dogs. Another reason is that dogs love to learn. Learning isn't a chore for them, it keeps them alert and focused.

Whether it's chasing birds away from airport runways, tracking big cats through their droppings or sniffing out poisonous toads, the reward for dogs engaged in these tasks is not the end result. It's the stimulation of the chase.

'Reward is important, but my concern is that nearly all the rewards given to dogs are of an external sort, such as biscuits. The important thing is to generate a sense of internal reward – 'I am doing this because I like doing it and it makes me happy' – that's where confidence comes from. What you really want is for the dog to enjoy learning for the pleasure of it.' DANIEL MILLS, PROFESSOR OF VETERINARY BEHAVIOURAL MEDICINE, LINCOLN UNIVERSITY

'I've had evenings where I'm packing for a work trip and I can't find Diesel. Then I'll find him sitting in the car waiting for me, eager to get on with his job.'
KELLY MARNEWICK, ENDANGERED WILDLIFE TRUST

NATURE TRAIL

The tracking abilities of Staffordshire Bull Terrier Diesel are helping to save endangered cheetahs in South Africa.

Capable of achieving speeds of an astonishing 114kmph (71mph), the cheetah is the fastest land animal on earth. Today, human encroachment on this magnificent cat's natural habitat is threatening its survival. Over the past 25 years, the South African cheetah population has halved to the point where only 250 breeding pairs remain. With numbers coming under ever greater pressure, the need for fast, efficient ways of assessing population size and tracking their movements is becoming more urgent.

Researchers at the Carnivore Conservation Programme, part of South Africa's Endangered Wildlife Trust (EWT), are working hard to save these big cats before it's too late. Aiding their efforts is a Staffordshire Bull Terrier called Diesel, whose amazing tracking abilities are proving invaluable.

Like many such endangered species, cheetahs are best tracked by their faecal droppings, known as scat. Analyzing scat allows researchers to identify not only species, but also sex and individual identities, crucial information required to estimate population size and distribution.

Kelly Marnewick, Diesel's handler, explains why he is such an asset: 'Using dogs for research just makes life so much easier. When we were running a research project on cheetahs on a reserve in the north of South Africa, we had researchers full time on the ground. On average they were taking something like 26 hours to find one scat.

When we brought Diesel along, he was averaging an hour a scat.'

Vim Foster, conservationist and researcher working at the Rietvlei Nature Reserve, agrees that it makes quite a difference. 'It always helps to have a Staffy like Diesel to give me a hand. In the summer, after the rain, the grass in the nature reserve is very high. And for me to walk through the grass looking for cheetah scats, it's basically like looking for a needle in a haystack.'

Diesel has been carefully trained to differentiate cheetah scat from the droppings of hundreds of other species. On the reserve he is walked across the direction of the wind so that he can pick up the scent in the air. The scent rises from the scat in a cone shape and he will zigzag back and forth inside this cone until he finds it.

Once a week Diesel goes to a training centre to ensure he stays on top of his game. Here canine trainer Shannon McKay presents Diesel with numerous different scats, only one of which has come from a cheetah. After Diesel correctly identifies the right one, he is given lots of praise – and a ball to play with. 'The ball is the way a terrier like Diesel gets to exercise his prey drive. I call it his behavioural itch,' says Shannon. 'It's really not that difficult to train a dog to use his nose – he does it every waking moment of his life. But it's fantastic to see dogs being used more and more in detection work.'

'*When Ozzie discovers the scent of a cane toad, his little tail wags, his ears prick up and he just goes ballistic.*'

KRYSTYNE LOVE, OZZIE'S HANDLER

ECO WARRIOR

Manchester Terrier Ozzie is an invaluabe weapon in the fight against Australia's destructive and poisonous cane toads.

Groote Eylandt is the largest island in an archipelago located in the Gulf of Carpentaria, 50km off the coast of Australia's Northern Territory. It's a unique and very precious environment, home to around 900 species of plants and 330 types of vertebrates. Ozzie, a Manchester Terrier, is helping it to stay that way.

One of the greatest potential threats to the island's fragile ecosystem is the poisonous cane toad. Cane toads, native to the Americas, were first introduced to Australia in a bid to control the beetles that were devouring Queensland's sugarcane fields. The toads proved unsuccessful at pest control. Instead, they turned into pests themselves, spreading into the Northern Territory and other areas, where over the years they have seriously affected biodiversity.

Anindilyakwa Land Council, which governs the island, wants to keep the toads out at all costs in order to protect this special habitat. That's why they have turned to Ozzie and his impressive instincts.

Manchester Terriers, originally bred as working dogs in the early nineteenth century, have a strong drive to hunt. Athletic and lithe, they're also short-haired and lightweight, which makes them ideal for working in the heat of the tropics.

Gary Jackson of Multi National K9 has taught Ozzie to detect the odour of cane toads. Ozzie is one of only three dogs in the world that have been trained for this job; these dogs can smell a live toad from a distance of 20m. But in the fight against cane toad invaders, his hunting instincts play as important a role as his keen nose. 'We don't just want him to detect where a cane toad's been,' says Gary. 'We want him to hunt down live toads that might have come over to the island in shipping containers.'

As a trained detection dog, Ozzie is able to track minimal changes in odour that indicate not only where a toad has been, but also where it is going. Odour concentration decreases with time and so more recent trails have a stronger scent than older ones. Using his superb sense of smell, Ozzie is able to reconstruct the path a toad might have taken.

Ozzie and his handler Kristyne Love have been working together on Groote Eylandt for eighteen months now, and have a very close relationship. As well as ensuring that the little dog is kept hydrated in these extreme conditions, Kristyne must also keep him permanently on the lead. Cane toads are so poisonous that if he were to chew one he might die.

Ozzie's impressive tracking instinct is ensuring that Groote Eylandt stays cane-toad free, and that this fragile eco-system will be safe for many generations to come.

FEELING THE HEAT

Inhospitable conditions can't stop a team of Australian dogs stemming the spread of the toxic red fire ant.

Native to South America, the red fire ant thrives in conditions of extreme heat. Capable of causing extensive damage to the environment, it also has a nasty sting whose toxic venom can be harmful to humans and livestock alike. Small wonder that when an outbreak of these unwelcome imports was discovered in Queensland, Australia, in 2001, a national programme was launched to prevent them from spreading to the rest of the country where they could pose a threat both to agriculture and tourism.

Biosecurity Queensland Control Centre (BQCC) is dedicated to the eradication of red fire ants. Assisting in this work is an incredible team of dogs from Brisbane, the first in the world to be trained in the detection of these introduced pests.

Red fire ants are hard to find. Humans have to rely on sighting the ant mounds to track them down. Dogs, however, are capable of sniffing out the distinctive scent these ants give off and can find their mounds – and even individual ants – fast. Accessing areas humans can't reach, they have increased detection rates by 60%.

But there's a problem about using these odour-detecting dogs. Fire ants are extremely aggressive, and they are as dangerous to dogs as they are to humans. Cara McNicol, operations manager of BQCC, explains: 'Fire ants aim for the soft tissue areas, eyes, nose, mouth and ears. They will attack en masse to deliver the maximum amount of toxins.'

Before dogs can be cleared for this hazardous work, they have to be screened. Under careful veterinary supervision, a fire ant is allowed to sting the dog on its nose to ensure the venom does not trigger an anaphylactic reaction.

An even greater challenge is the extreme conditions under which the dogs have to operate. In the arid heat of the desert and shrub lands of Queensland, temperatures regularly reach 40°C.

A dog's normal body temperature averages 38.9°C. In hot conditions it can rise rapidly and lead to heat stroke. If a few minutes in a baking car is enough to threaten a dog's life, how do these dogs cope with the task in hand? Adam Bean, dog handler, explains: 'We cool the dogs with fans when they're resting. We also strap ice vests across their chests to lower their core body temperature. But it also depends on the dog. Half of the dogs in the team are black Labs and because they heat up more quickly due to their colour we don't let them search as long in the sun as some of our paler dogs.'

When the temperature rises to over 40°C, the dogs are only worked for 15 minutes at a time, before they are led away to rest and cool down. Even so, a typical day will see the dogs out in the field for a four-hour period. That takes extraordinary stamina.

Great care is taken of the dogs working for BQCC as they search for red fire ants in Queensland's fierce heat. The extreme temperatures mean that the dogs can only hunt for limited periods.

'Towards the end of the summer the dogs end up very, very fit because they've been working in tough, extreme conditions. Only animals with high levels of stamina can do this kind of work.'

ADAM BEAN, DOG HANDLER

Tina and Melissa on airport patrol.

'The dogs love their job. They're absolutely in their element on airside.'
MELISSA HOFFMAN, ACSA WILDLIFE CONTROL OFFICER FOR O.R. TAMBO INTERNATIONAL AIRPORT

READY FOR TAKE-OFF

Without harming avian wildlife, Border Collies Scott and Tina make Johannesburg's international airport safe from bird strike.

The potentially disastrous consequences of bird strike worry many in the aviation industry. Simple collisions between birds and planes generally carry no risk to passengers. If a bird gets sucked into an engine, however, it can cause it to fail, leading to a crash of catastrophic proportions.

O.R. Tambo International Airport in Johannesburg, like many around the world, occupies a wide, open area in close proximity to water. Tall grasses that grow on the site are home to many species of wildlife, most of which pose no threat to air traffic. But the environment is also attractive for many birds.

Border Collies Scott and Tina are two of the special dogs being deployed at South Africa's airports in a pioneering form of bird control. They work as part of the Bird Strike Avoidance Programme, set up by the Endangered Wildlife Trust (EWT). Every day for three years, Scott and Tina have chased birds from the runways at O.R. Tambo Airport with their handler Melissa Hoffman. The idea is not to harm the birds, or catch them, but to discourage them from the site. 'If a bird cannot breed or feed successfully in an area, it will move off. We use a potential predator to put pressure on the birds and reduce the numbers on the airfield,' says Melissa.

Border Collies are highly intelligent, adaptable working dogs. They are also very focused, which means they respond well to complex training. Scott and Tina have had two years of specialized teaching during which they learned to respond to different whistle commands.

As they accompany Melissa on her quad bike, touring the expanses of the airport, a continuous whistle tells them when to jump off the bike and go and chase birds. A short whistle is the signal to lie down because an aircraft is nearby. Another, different, whistle command calls them back to the bike. 'It's surprising but aircraft noise doesn't distract them from their job. They're not sound shy,' says Melissa. 'They don't react even if a plane is departing or landing 50 metres from them. When they see a bird, their main focus is the bird.'

Like many dogs bred as herders, Border Collies instinctively react to peripheral visual stimuli and can detect movement over great distances. The flat vistas of the airfield exploit Scott and Tina's keen visual powers to the full. Together with Melissa, the collies can control birds over a vast territory – up to 50km/30 miles and beyond. Over the years a special bond has grown between them, with the dogs learning their handler's body language and behaviour patterns so well they are often able to anticipate when they should get ready to jump off the bike.

For these dogs, the fun is all in the chase. 'Their reward is to see the birds fly away,' says Melissa. 'We don't offer food rewards. It's basically the chase that stimulates them.'

8

On the
Front Line

On the Front Line

Meet the professionals. Whether patrolling combat zones around the world, assisting police track down criminals or detecting dangerous or illegal substances, time after time dogs have clearly demonstrated they have what it takes to be on the front line.

ON GUARD

Defensive roles are nothing new for dogs, which are instinctively loyal and protective of their fellow pack members. Ever since dogs joined forces with humans, they have been valued for their willingness to stand guard and ward off predators. A mosaic floor in the ruins of a house in Pompeii spelling out the message *Cave canem* ('Beware of the dog') shows that the effectiveness of dogs as deterrents to intruders has been appreciated for thousands of years.

Contrary to popular belief, good guard dogs are not aggressive. Aggression is a complex behaviour trait in a dog and one that often indicates poor training (or lack of it), previous maltreatment or fear. Instead, well-trained guard dogs display a confident assertiveness, employing scare tactics such as growling, staring and intimidating body postures to threaten rather than harm. Their bark is literally worse than their bite.

DOG DETECTIVES

While canines have worked as protectors, trackers and guardians of the peace for many years, it was not until after the Second World War that they became more widely involved in official police work. At the end of the nineteenth century, a new breed developed in Germany, the German Shepherd dog, proved to have excellent qualities for police duty and it remains one of the most popular breeds for patrol work, along with the Belgian Malinois, which closely resembles it.

Today thousands of dogs assist the police in their inquiries all over the world, some as bodyguards and deterrents, some as canine detectives, sniffing out the evidence that will lead to convictions. 'Sniffer dogs' are chosen from breeds and stock that can use their natural sense of smell efficiently, such as Spaniels, Beagles and Labradors. Working to detect explosives, drugs, pirated goods and other illegal substances, these extraordinary canines have proved themselves to be the ultimate weapon in the war against crime.

DOGS OF WAR

In ancient times, giant mastiffs, kitted out with armour and spiked collars, would be sent into battle, fighting alongside their masters. More recently, major conflicts have seen dogs used as hauliers, messengers, rescuers and mascots.

Today, dogs in the military fulfil a number of different roles. Patrol dogs in the forces are deemed a 'sub-lethal force', trained not to kill, but to attack the right arm of their target where, 90 per cent of the time, the weapon will be carried. On patrol, their exceptional senses help prevent security breaches, while their large jaws and strong muscular physique serve as a powerful deterrent. Equally important are the detection dogs, trained to uncover roadside bombs and other explosive devices, to detect hidden weapons and to clear suspect locations.

'Dogs have an amazing ability to teach themselves. When we train a dog to track scent, the dog does a lot of self-training. There's a good deal we don't understand about scent detection.'

DANIEL MILLS, PROFESSOR OF
VETERINARY BEHAVIOURAL MEDICINE,
LINCOLN UNIVERSITY

'I've been working with JC for two years so we're pretty close. She knows me really well. Very few verbal commands are necessary. She knows what to do.'

CORPORAL SARANIERO,
US MARINE CORPS

Their intelligence, strength and abilities in obedience training make German Shepherds, like US Marine Corps dog JC, the number one dog employed by military and police forces around the world.

'Before Paddy arrived, we just relied on the information we had. There could be millions' worth of DVDs hidden in a warehouse and we could miss it. Now his sense of smell guides us through the whole process. Dogs don't lie, they can't mislead you. They just follow their senses.'

SHANKSAR, HEAD OF THE K-9 UNIT

CRIME-BUSTER

Labrador Paddy's extraordinary detective skills are integral to the Malaysian authorities' fight against film piracy.

Film piracy is a serious crime that costs the movie industry a fortune in lost revenue. It's particularly rife in countries in the Asia Pacific Region where, according to the Moving Picture Association of America, disc and Internet piracy leads to a staggering loss of $1.2 billion every year.

Black Labrador Paddy is one of three dogs trained to detect the odour of polycarbonate, a chemical used in the manufacture of DVDs. He works in Malaysia as part of a dedicated canine anti-piracy team, the K-9 Unit of the Enforcement Division of the Ministry of Domestic Trade, Co-operatives and Consumerism (MDTCC).

Paddy was trained in Ireland, the first country where dogs have been used to combat piracy. Now his extraordinary detection skills are being put to the test halfway around the world in the fight against this lucrative crime. The results so far have been amazing.

When the Malaysian authorities believe that a warehouse or shopfront conceals an illegal disc-duplication operation or caches of pirated discs, Paddy and his handler Michael will be called upon to determine whether their suspicions are correct. If Paddy confirms that DVDs are present at the location, the MDTCC will then go in and raid the premises.

An early success came in 2009 when the MDTCC carried out a big raid on a suspect location. With Paddy's assistance, they were able to seize a massive haul of pirated CDs and DVDs hidden in a maze of tunnels.

For Shanksar, head of the K-9 Unit, Paddy's work has been invaluable. Before the dogs arrived, investigative teams would often be going into situations blind. 'When Paddy goes to a place and gets a whiff of a scent, he will quickly sit. The moment he sits is a positive indication that there is illegal material,' says Shanksar.

Paddy's sense of smell is so astoundingly good he can even detect DVDs through locked steel doors. As part of his on-going training, his handler Michael regularly hides DVDs for him to find. 'I really care about him,' says Michael. 'He's just like one of us, he's like a brother.'

In their first six months on the job the team have helped the Malaysian authorities unearth 1.6 million pirated DVDs and other optical discs and equipment worth more than £3 million.

The K-9 unit has proved so successful at crime-busting that one pirate syndicate is rumoured to have put a bounty of $30,000 on the dogs' heads. As a result, the location of their training centre and base has to be kept top secret.

FIREMAN SAM

Detecting skills run in the family of Springer Spaniel Sam, whose capabilities are superior to any on-site piece of fire investigating equipment.

The seaside resort of Eastbourne on the south coast of England is home to around 100,000 people. It's also the home of one of the country's leading fire investigators, whose work has led to the arrest of numerous arsonists.

Meet Sam, an exceptional English Springer Spaniel. Sam is a member of the Arson and Incident Reduction Team at East Sussex Fire and Rescue Service. He's trained to search the scene of a fire to determine whether any flammable liquids have been involved in the incident. Sarah Jones, Watch Manager at the Arson and Incident Reduction Team, is Sam's handler and they handle about three call-outs a month. 'Sam plays a vital role within the fire investigation team,' says Sarah. 'He's able to detect minute amounts of flammable liquid at a scene, something no other piece of equipment available to the investigators can do.'

When firefighters suspect arson, Sam's job is to sniff out any flammable liquids that might have been used to start the fire or accelerate it. In the aftermath of a house fire, that's no easy task. Yet Sam can get results much faster than taking samples back to a lab for analysis.

All dogs have a keen sense of smell, which is up to 10,000 times more powerful than our own for some odours, and even higher for others. Spaniels, originally bred as gun dogs, have particularly good noses, which they use in the field to scent and flush out game. Today, they are often called upon to be sniffer dogs like Sam.

Key to Sam's success is rigorous and on-going training. Sarah explains: 'We keep Sam's sense of smell at its best by continuation and development training. We get out as often as possible and make the searches as varied and as complicated as we can.' Sam is taught to detect the difference between naturally occurring hydrocarbons that you would expect to find after a fire, and those produced by an accelerant that has been introduced to the scene.

His sense of smell is so acute that, presented with five pans containing burnt materials commonly found in house fires, such as charred wood and polystyrene, he is able to correctly identify the one that has been contaminated with a single drop of 'odourless' white spirit. The only times he runs into difficulties is when large quantities of fuel have been used. 'If it's possible for you or me to smell fuel, he would have trouble because the smell's so overwhelming,' says Sarah.

Training helps keep Sam up to the mark. But his outstanding qualities also run in the family. Both his parents are trained sniffer dogs. His mother works in drug detection and his father detects explosives.

Sam keeps up his skills with on-going training, checking samples of burnt material to find the one contaminated with fire accelerant.

'Without Sam we wouldn't be able to tell the difference between the hydrocarbons that occur naturally through combustion and those produced by flammable liquids. There's no piece of equipment available to fire investigation officers that could otherwise be used on a site.'

SARAH JONES, WATCH MANAGER, ARSON AND INCIDENT REDUCTION TEAM, EAST SUSSEX FIRE AND RESCUE SERVICE

FIGHTING FIT

For US military and police force dogs, like German Shepherd JC, a tough Hawaiian competition is a combination of strenuous training and fun.

Schofield Barracks on the island of Oahu, Hawaii, home of the US Army 25th Infantry Division, is the location of an annual competition to test the agility and staying power of dogs working in the police and armed forces. Dogs and their handlers vie to win the ultimate accolade of 'Hardest Hitting Dog' in one of the toughest and most respected competitions around.

In 2010, thirty-seven teams from across the Pacific and continental United States came together to demonstrate their exceptional skills and share their training techniques. One such competitor was JC, a German Shepherd who works on patrol with the United States Marine Corps as an explosive detector dog. Her handler is Corporal Saraniero. 'I joined this competition as a chance to showcase the level of dogs that we have,' he says. 'The Marine Corps pride themselves on being the best at everything. This gives us the opportunity to see what the other services are doing. The competition is also good for the dogs because it puts them in situations they aren't normally faced with and really tests their capabilities as working dogs.'

Sergeant McPeak, the organizer of the competition, explains the rationale behind the event: 'This is a test of physical fitness and cohesiveness in the dog team and of the dog's willingness to negotiate different tasks in the shortest possible time. Both handler and dog need a lot of agility and endurance.'

In some breeds of dog, nearly 60 percent of their body is muscle. This makes them ideal animals for defence and operational work. Risking their lives alongside humans in combat zones all over the world, the dogs' stamina and agility are regularly put to the test. All the more so, as many will be required to wear protective vests, armour that adds extra weight to their body mass.

Competitions such as these are not simply about winning the coveted title. They also allow the dogs to improve their skills and thus provide the military with far more capable working animals. While many of the task and assault courses appear strenuous and difficult, the dogs gain an immense amount of enjoyment from the work. For them each test is a game that will bring rewards if performed correctly.

During the competition, JC and her handler Corporal Saraniero clearly demonstrated that all the training had paid off. They won two awards, one for the obedience course and one for explosive detection. 'It was a blast,' says Corporal Saraniero. 'I had a lot of fun and my dog enjoyed it too. It's all a game for her. I was very proud to win the obedience award. I came out there a little hesitant of some of the obstacles, but performed to the best of my ability and my dog performed to the best of her ability and we walked away with a trophy.'

Military dogs show their levels of fitness negotiating the 'Hardest Hitting Dog' course

Comfort,
Love &
Loyalty

Comfort, Love & Loyalty

Cesky Terriers (*left*) are so immensely loyal to their families that, despite their small size, they make excellent house guards. The Bassett hound (*right*) is extremely affectionate, with a gentle disposition.

Humans and dogs enjoy an extraordinary bond. Ever since dogs were domesticated, 15,000 years ago, we have benefitted from their comfort, loyalty and love, just as dogs have grown to depend on us for their survival. Over the centuries this bond has only deepened as we have selectively bred dogs for their willingness to respond to us and work with us.

ONE OF THE FAMILY

The instinctive loyalty of dogs lies deep within their genetic makeup. Dogs share 99.8% of their genes with wolves, from which they are directly descended. Wolves organize themselves in social units or family-oriented packs, consisting of a mated pair, biological offspring and adopted subordinates. Yet while wolves have remained aloof from humankind, the process of domestication has taught dogs to transfer their loyalty to members of their adopted human families.

SPECIAL RELATIONSHIP

It is thought that dogs initiated the process of domestication themselves. The beginning of the relationship probably occurred when less fearful wolves were attracted by the scavenging possibilities offered by the rubbish dumps near early settlements, and in the process grew closer to humans.

Through domestication, the paths of dogs and wolves gradually diverged. 'One of the things that seems to distinguish a dog from a wolf is the dog's ability to form stable reciprocal relationships with humans,' explains Daniel Mills, Profession of Veterinary Behavioural Medicine, Lincoln University. 'You could never trust a wolf, no matter how much time you spent with it. Dogs, on the other hand, are less aggressive and tend to be much more loyal and consistent in that loyalty.'

TALES OF DEVOTION

Legendary tales of dogs' loyalty abound. In nineteenth-century Edinburgh a little Skye terrier called Greyfriars Bobby stood guard over the grave of his master for fourteen years, an act of devotion honoured after the dog's death by a statue being raised to him. In a suburb of Tokyo, another statue commemorates the amazing love and faithfulness of Hachiko, a Japanese Akita, who in the 1930s continued to wait every evening to meet his master's commuter train at Shibuya station – twelve years after his beloved owner had died.

THE FEEL-GOOD FACTOR

There are clear physiological reasons why dogs have the ability to comfort us and make us feel better. Studies have shown that stroking a dog releases oxytocin in the brain, a chemical sometimes known as the 'love hormone'. Oxytocin, which operates as a neurotransmitter, has the effect of making us feel more content, less anxious and more secure. It is thought that when we stroke our dogs, levels of oxytocin are raised both in us and in our pets. But as Dr Bruce Fogle, canine expert, explains: 'It doesn't necessarily happen when you stroke someone else's dog. It's much more marked when you are stroking a dog you've formed a relationship with.'

'Dogs have co-evolved with humans, so building up a close relationship with us has been key to their survival.'

DANIEL MILLS, PROFESSOR OF
VETERINARY BEHAVIOURAL
MEDICINE, LINCOLN UNIVERSITY

Newfoundlands love water and they love children, facts that charity Newfound Friends has put to good use, with children like Christopher (*below*) who are learning water rescue techniques with big friendly giant Whizz.

GENTLE GIANT

The love and protectiveness that Newfoundland Whizz shows children with learning difficulties has made a big difference to the life of ten-year-old Christopher.

Friendly and sociable, the huge Newfoundland dog is known for its affection for people and its willingness to work. But two characteristics, in particular, distinguish this breed from almost all other types of dog – their affinity with water and the great love and protectiveness they instinctively show towards children. Both are clearly demonstrated by a very special Newfoundland called Whizz, an experienced water rescue dog who also provides therapeutic assistance for children with learning difficulties.

Whizz's owner, David Pugh, is the founder of Bristol-based charity Newfound Friends, originally set up in 1990 to use the skills of Newfoundland dogs to raise money for children's causes. He explains that there are lots of stories about the special bond between these gentle giants and children much smaller than they are. 'Years ago ships' captains sailing across the Atlantic would often bring back a Newfoundland and actually use the dog as a nanny.'

One of the programmes run by Newfound Friends is the Rookie Lifeguard scheme, which brings dogs like Whizz together with children like Christopher, a ten year old with learning difficulties. Every Sunday, Christopher gets into his wet suit and learns basic water rescue techniques with Whizz. 'An animal trainer in the making,' says David

Pugh, paricularly impressed by the presence and authority Christopher shows around the huge dogs.

For a child with learning difficulties any activity that promotes social skills and physical development is invaluable. But Christopher clearly gets so much more out of his interaction with Whizz. Right from the beginning his parents Andy and Rachael noticed the difference. 'We didn't realize it would have such an amazing effect. Christopher gets so excited knowing that we're going there on a Sunday to meet the dogs and all his new friends. Even though he's going to be pulled through the freezing cold water, he enjoys it and gets so much out of it.' When they aren't training in the water, that positive influence is still apparent. 'He has a bond with the dogs I've not seen with other animals before,' says mum Rachel. 'They are four or five times his size and he has no fear of them at all. Whizz is so calming and quiet. Christopher will stay still to sit with him, which is unusual.'

This doesn't surprise David Pugh, who is a firm believer in the benefits of bringing children with difficulties together with dogs. The charity now takes Newfoundlands into hospices where their steady, loving natures and innate compassion for people in distress gives another dimension to the care of those with uncertain futures.

PUPPY LOVE

Australian prisoners learn valuable life skills by training puppies to become assistance dogs and are rewarded with love and a new sense of purpose.

Preparing puppies to become assistance dogs takes a lot of time and dedication, more than most busy families have to spare in their daily lives. When Assistance Dogs Australia (ADA) started running short of volunteers prepared to raise their puppies, they turned to a very different type of community, where people have plenty of time on their hands: prison.

ADA's innovative 'Pups in Prison' programme now places puppies with inmates in correctional facilities all over the country. Prisoners are carefully selected to join the programme and receive weekly lessons from ADA trainers to show them how to teach their pups the skills they will need as active service dogs. But from the time the pups arrive at the age of about eight weeks to when they leave a year later the bulk of the training is done by their inmate handlers.

The Ron Barwick Minimum Security Prison in Hobart, Tasmania, is the latest facility to join the programme. Home to 125 male inmates, the jail has a history of violence and riots. Correctional Manager Robert McCafferty admits the authorities were sceptical at first, particularly as prisoners would have to be let out after curfew so their puppies could go to the toilet. Now he has been completely won over. 'Prior to the programme, some inmates wouldn't make eye contact with you. Now they do. They're standing taller and their communication

skills are improving. For the first time in their lives they feel responsible for something.'

Frachie is a seven-and-a-half-month old Labrador pup. From the moment she wakes up, her day is filled with exercises – wheelchair work, retrieving dropped objects, all the basic training she will need as a service dog. But she's not the only one learning new skills. For her inmate trainer, the experience has been transforming. 'In most prisons you focus on negative things. It's good to have something positive to focus on every day. This programme has changed my outlook on a lot of things. It's taught me about teamwork and patience and given me life skills.' He originally signed up to the programme because he had witnessed the daily struggles of his son-in-law, who has cerebral palsy, and had been unable to help the way he wanted to. Now the programme has even changed his attitude to the prison system as a whole. 'Knowing they're willing to give this a go in here is a sort of reinforcement that we're not just here to be punished, we can do something good.'

The prisoners have turned out to be the perfect trainers for the pups, with plenty of time to give them the full attention they require. At the same time, the love the dogs give their inmate trainers, along with the prisoners' new-found sense of responsibility, are proving to have a huge impact on rates of reform.

'The healing power of animals within a prison system
is underestimated and probably untried as to its
fullest potential.'

ROBERT MCCAFFERTY, MANAGER OF RON BARWICK MINIMUM
SECURITY PRISON, HOBART

IN THE NICK OF TIME

Showing incredible intelligence and loyalty,
Buddy the German Shepherd ran for help and
led police to a dangerous fire at his owner's
home in Alaska.

Over the years, the remarkable bond between dog and human has been demonstrated in many tales of loyalty and devotion. Time and again, dogs have gone to extraordinary lengths to protect their adopted families in times of danger or threat. A potentially catastrophic event that took place last year in Alaska proved to be one such occasion.

Ben Heinrichs lives with his family and his German Shepherd, Buddy, in Caswell Lakes, a remote region of the state. As he often did in the early evening, Ben was in his shed fixing his truck when a spark ignited some gasoline and started a fire.

Ben's first instinct was to get himself out of the shed and close the door behind him to hold the fire in check. After he put out his burning clothing, he realized his dog was still in the shed and hurried back to let him out. 'That's when I said "We need to find help." I ran and Buddy took off. I didn't see where he went.'

State Trooper Shanigan was on the highway about five miles north of the property when he got a frantic call from one of the Heinrichs' neighbours, saying there was a fire at her friend's house and that someone had been hurt. But as he left the highway and headed for the house, the GPS in his car stopped working. With 150km of backroads crisscrossing the region, one wrong turn could have meant getting lost for hours. There was nothing to do but to wait for directions to come through from the control room.

It was when he was slowly approaching a four-way intersection, wondering which direction to turn, that he noticed something out of the corner of his eye. As he pulled round a corner, he saw a German Shepherd in the road. At the sight of the car the dog began to sprint in front, barking persistently. 'From that point on, I never really thought twice,' says Trooper Shanigan. 'I just went with my gut feeling and followed him.'

Buddy led the trooper straight to the fire, where the policeman promptly called the fire trucks and ambulance. It was just in the nick of time. The shed, full of highly inflammable materials, and close to a propane tank, could have blown up at any moment and the fire spread to the house. Ben and his mother Lynette could hardly believe their ears when they heard what Buddy had done. 'Honestly,' says Ben, 'I don't know what would have happened if it wasn't for him. We could have lost everything.'

'Buddy's very loyal. You can tell that just by the way he interacts with Ben and the family. On that day, for that minute and a half, Buddy let me into something that he and Ben probably experience more often. I don't know if Buddy knows the significance of what he's done, but he definitely has special qualities I don't see in a lot of dogs.'

TROOPER SHANIGAN

 # A WINNING TEAM

The unshakeable bond of love and loyalty between young Amy Rouse and Mist, her Border Collie, has led to remarkable success in the world of sheepdog trialling.

All dogs are naturally group-orientated, instinctively loyal to those they perceive as members of their immediate family. In human households, they project the role of 'parent' onto the one who predominantly feeds them, walks them, plays with them and scolds them. Most dogs are also highly intelligent, capable of learning many different skills and commands. Put this innate sense of loyalty together with good training and you've got a dog with the potential to go far.

Fifteen-year-old Amy Rouse and her clever Border Collie Mist make an unbeatable combination. In the highly competitive world of sheepdog trials, they are already making their mark, confounding old hands with decades' worth of experience. Amy is

not only the youngest ever contender in the history of the English National Sheepdog Trials, she's also a young woman in a sport dominated by much older men, which makes her achievements doubly impressive. The basis for her success is the amazing bond she shares with her beloved Collie.

According to canine expert Professor Daniel Mills, puppies form social ties early: 'Dogs go through a socialization period soon after birth. They can start to form close relationships any time from about two weeks onwards. At this point, humans start to form part of the social world of the dog.'

The bond between Amy and her dog began from the moment Mist was born. Amy's father, Andrew, competes in trials himself

and Mist's mother was one of his dogs. As soon as Mist and her littermates were old enough to walk, Amy noticed that the puppy liked to follow her about. 'She'd be by my feet and wherever I'd go, she'd shadow me. She's always been with me and around me.' Amy's mother Janet agrees. 'They don't like being apart.'

Four years later, the remarkable obedience Mist shows in competitions is the product of that loyalty as much as all the hours of training that Amy has put in teaching her dog to respond to both verbal and whistle commands. Amy won her first sheepdog trial two years ago. 'She just walked it,' her father says. 'In fact, she won every one of the first

six trials. It's just unbelievable.'

Since then the pair have gone from strength to strength. Last year they competed in the novice class in the prestigious Wayland Agricultural Show in Norfolk and swept to glory. Now, within six months of moving into the Opens from novice level, they have gained top points for entry into the National Competitions, an extraordinary feat for such a young team.

Best of all, perhaps, is a very special honour. Amy has recently won the title of England's Young Handler, which means that she and Mist represented their country in the International Young Handlers competition.

'Amy and Mist are a terrific partnership. They've got this bond between them, this total understanding. If you can get that in sheepdog trialling, then you've pretty much got the key to unlock the whole game.'

FRED CHAPMAN,
FELLOW SHEEPDOG TRIALLIST

'Some trialling people treat their dogs like they're work tools, whereas I treat my dog like she's my best friend. Mist means everything to me.'

AMY ROUSE

Organizations

The Publishers would like to thank the following organizations featured in the book

Altitude 5000 Sled Dog Race
(Black Dog Sled Dog Team)
Dinner Plain, Victoria
Australia
www.sleddogchallenge.com

The Mira Foundation Inc
(Fondation MIRA)
1820 Rang Nord Ouest
Ste Madeleine
Quebec J0H 1S0
Canada
www.mira.ca

**School of Guide Dogs for the Blind and Visually
Impaired of Paris and RP**
(Ecole de Chiens Guides d'Aveugles de Paris et
de la Region Parisienne)
105 Avenue St Maurice
Paris F-75012
France
www.paris.chiensguides.fr

Japan Guide Dog Association (JGDA)
Kanagawa Training School
6001-9, Shin-Yoshida-cho, Kohoku-ku,
Yokohama-shi,
Kanagawa 223-0056
Japan
www.moudouken.net

Canine Companions for Independence, CCI
1-866-CCI-DOGS (224-3647)
P.O. Box 446
Santa Rosa, CA 95402-0446
USA
 www.cci.org

Hearing Dogs for Deaf People
The Grange, Wycombe Road
Saunderton, Princes Risborough
Buckinghamshire, HP27 9NS
UK
www.hearingdogs.org.uk

Guiding Eyes for the Blind
611 Granite Springs Rd
Yorktown Heights, NY 10598
USA
www.guidingeyes.org

Cancer and Bio-detection Dogs
Unit 3, Millfield
Greenway Business Park
Winslow Road, Great Horwood
Nr. Milton Keynes, MK17 0NP
UK
www.cancerdogs.co.uk
www.hypoalertdogs.co.uk

Hachiko vzw
Hundelgemsesteenweg 722
8920 Merelbeke
Belgium
www.hachiko.org

National Service Dogs (NSD)
PO Box 28009 Preston Postal Outlet
Cambridge, ON N3H 5N4
Canada
www.nsd.on.ca

University of Otago
Department of Psychology
Box 56, Dunedin
New Zealand
www.otago.ac.nz

The Pines Nursing Home
3015 17th Street NW
Canton, OH 44708
USA
www.atriumlivingcenters.com

Eötvös Loránd University - ELTE
Egyetem tér 1-3
Budapest, 1053
Hungary

The Italian School of Water Rescue Dogs
(Scuola Italiana Cani Salvataggio – SICS)
Milano Idroscalo
Italy
www.waterrescuedogs.com

New Zealand Land Search & Rescue (LandSAR)
Level 2, 276 Lambton Quay
P O Box 25-362, Wellington 6146
New Zealand
www.landsar.org.nz
New Zealand Urban Search & Rescue
www.usar.govt.nz

Unidad Canina de Rescate y Salvamento Ong K9
Ezeiza
Argentina
(UNRS)

Rescue Dog Trainer's Association (RDTA)
Japan
www.rdta.or.jp
www.iro-dogs.org

Endangered Wildlife Trust (EWT)
Private Bag X11, Parkview 2122
South Africa
www.ewt.org.za

McKaynine Training Centre
(South Africa)
www.mckaynine.co.za

Anindilyakwa Land Council
Groote Eylandt, Northern Territory
Australia
www.anindilyakwa.com.au

Multi National K9
P.O. Box 535, Kallangur
Queensland 4503
Australia

Biosecurity Queensland Control Centre (BQCC)
Australia
www.dpi.qld.gov.au

Ministry of Domestic Trade, Co-operatives and Consumerism (MDTCC)
Malaysia
www.malaysia.gov.my

East Sussex Fire and Rescue Service
20 Upperton Rd, Eastbourne
East Sussex BN21 1EU
UK
www.esfrs.org

US 728th Military Police Battalion
US 8th Military Police Brigade
US Marine Corps Kaneohe Bay, Hawaii
USA
www.mcbh.usmc.mil

Newfound Friends
Days Cottage, Clevedon Lane
Clapton-in-Gordano BS20 7RH
UK
www.newfoundfriends.co.uk

Assistance Dogs Australia
PO Box 455, Engadine NSW 2233
Australia
www.assistancedogs.org.au

Ron Barwick Minimum Security Prison
East Derwent Highway
Risdon Vale, Tas 7015
Australia

The Publishers would like to thank the following experts for their contributions

Luca Ferasin
DVM PhD CertVC DipECVIM-CA (Cardiology)
MRCVS
Specialist Veterinary Cardiology Consultancy, Berkshire

Bruce Fogle
MBE DVM MRCVS
Canine expert

Christine Heinrich
DVOphthal DipECVO MRCVS
Willows Veterinary Centre and Referral Service, Solihull
Specialist in veterinary ophthalmology

John Innes
BVSc PhD CertVR DSAS(Orth) MRCVS
Professor of Small Animal Surgery
University of Liverpool School of Veterinary Science
Specialist in canine orthopaedics

Daniel S Mills
BVSc PhD CBiol FIBiol FHEA CCAB DipECVBM-CA
MRCVS
Professor of Veterinary Behavioural Medicine
Lincoln University
Specialist in veterinary behavioural medicine

David Morgan
BSc MA VetMB CertVR MRCVS
Eukanuba Scientific Communication Manager
Specialist in canine nutrition and health

Tim Nuttall
BSc BVSc CertVD PhD CBiol MSB MRCVS
The University of Liverpool School of Veterinary Science
Senior Lecturer in Veterinary Dermatology

Karen L. Overall,
MA,VMD PhD DiplACVB CAAB
Center for Neurobiology and Behavior
University of Pennsylvania School of Medicine
Specialist in animal behaviour

Karol Sikora
MA MBBCh PhD FRCR FRCP FFPM
Dean of the Medical School
University of Buckingham
Consultant Oncologist and former Professor of Cancer Medicine, Hammersmith Hospital, London

Photography
The publishers would like to thank Back2Back Productions, A Brand Apart Television and Procter and Gamble International Operations (photographer Françoise Nicaise) for the images used in the book.

INDEX

Entries in bold indicate photographs

Text Elizabeth Wilhide

Editorial director Anne Furniss
Creative director Helen Lewis
Project editor Sarah Mitchell
Designer Nicola Davidson
Editorial assistant Louise McKeever
Production director Vincent Smith
Production controller James Finan

First published in 2011 by
Quadrille Publishing Limited
Alhambra House
27–31 Charing Cross Road
London WC2H 0LS
www.quadrille.co.uk

Cataloguing in Publication Data: a catalogue record for this
book is available from the British Library.

ISBN 978 184949 000 9

Printed in Italy